Houghton Mifflin

Atlas of
American
History

RAND McNALLY

Project Manager
Carole Wicklander

Book Production Editor
Louise Frederiksen

Map Production Editor
Charles J. MacDonald

Managing Editor
Margaret McNamara

Digital Cartographers
Barbara Benstead-Strassheim
Elizabeth A. Hunt
Amy L. Troesch

Digital Cartography Project Manager
Thomas Vitacco

Cartographic Editorial
Robert K. Argersinger
Gregory P. Babiak
Jill M. Stift

Cartographic Production
Norma Denny
Jim Purvis

Manual Cartography Project Manager
David Zapenski

Designer
Donna McGrath

Production Manager
Robert Sanders

Typesetting
Yvonne Rosenberg

Photo Credit
Images provided by ©1999 PhotoDisc, Inc.

Copyright © 1999 by Rand McNally & Company

Printed in the United States of America

Rand McNally & Company
Skokie, Illinois 60076-8906

  456789-RM-05-04-03-02-

ISBN 528-84500-4

For information about ordering *Atlas of American History*, call 1-800-678-7263, or visit our website at www.k12online.com.

Table of Contents

Introduction 5

Section 1: Beginnings (prehistory-1620) 9

Early Routes and Cultures in the Americas

Routes of the First Americans,
23,000 - 8,000 B.C. 10

Viking Voyages, A.D. 1000 10

Where Native Americans Lived 11

European Trade Routes

International Trade, 1350-1450 12

Portuguese Routes to India, 1488-1498 13

Spanish and English Explorers

The Spanish in the Americas, 1492-1542 . . . 14

Cabot's Voyages, 1497-1498 15

England Searches for a
Northwest Passage, 1576-1586 15

French Explorers

Voyages of Cartier and Verrazano,
1524-1536 16

Explorations of Champlain and Brulé,
1603-1615 16

Section 2: Establishing Colonies (1600-1775) 17

Settling the Atlantic Coast

English Land Grants, 1606 18

Dutch and Swedish Settlements,
1623-1643 18

Plymouth Colony, 1620 19

Early Settlements in New England,
1620-1630 19

Expansion of New England, 1636-1640 . . . 19

Struggle for the North American Continent

French Influence in North America, 1682 . . 20

The Thirteen Original British Colonies,
1750 21

French and Indian War

French and British Forts, 1753-1760 22

British Strategy in the French and
Indian War, 1754-1763 22

North America, 1763 23

Colonial Economy

Sources of Wealth in the British
Colonies, 1770 24

Triangular Trade Routes, about 1770 24

Section 3: Forming a New Nation (1775-1800) 25

The Struggle for Independence

The Battles of Lexington and
Concord, 1775 26

The War in New England, 1775-1776 26

The Retreat from New York, 1776-1777 . . . 26

Clark's Route, 1778-1779 26

Northern Campaigns, 1777 27

The War in the South, 1780-1781 27

The Final Campaign, 1781 27

The Growing Republic

North America, 1783 28

Spanish Influence in North America,
late 1700s 28

State Claims to Western Lands 29

The United States, 1775-1800 29

Developing New States

The Northwest Territory, 1787 30

Section 4: The Nation Expands & Changes (1790-1870) 31

Expanding Through Treaties, Purchase, and War

British Held Posts, 1794 32

Louisiana Purchase, 1803, and
Its Exploration, 1804-1807 32

Campaigns in the War of 1812 33

The United States in 1819 33

Changes in the West and the East

Routes to the West,
about 1840 34

The Mexican War,
1846-1848 34

National Road and Canals, about 1840 35

The Removal of the
Eastern Indians, 1840 35

Acquiring New Territories

Westward Expansion, 1800-1850 36

Acquiring New Settlers

Major Sources of Immigration,
1820-1870 38

Section 5: A Nation Divided (1850-1865) 39

The Slavery Issue

The Compromise of 1850 40

Kansas-Nebraska Act, 1854 40

Slaves and the Underground Railroad, about 1860 40

A Quarreling People, 1820-1860 41

The Civil War

Secession, 1860-1861 42

The Civil War 43

Major Civil War Battles

The Civil War, 1861-1865 44

1861-1863 44

1864-1865 44

Section 6: Emerging as a Modern Nation (1860-1920) 45

Expansion and Involvement Beyond the Mainland

Western Frontiers, 1860-1890 46

Expansion Overseas, 1865-1920 47

Spanish-American War in Cuba, 1898 47

Spanish-American War in the Philippines, 1898 47

The New Immigrants

Major Sources of Immigration, 1880-1920 48

Immigration's Impact, 1910 49

World War I

World War I, Europe in 1914 50

The Western Front in 1918 50

Section 7: Challenges & Changes in the 20th Century (1920-1990) 51

Economic Growth and Depression

United States Industries, 1920 52

Great Depression, 1929-1939 53

World War II: Axis Expansion

World War II, The Height of Axis Expansion, 1942 54

World War II: Allied Advances

World War II, 1941-1945 Pacific Theater ... 56

World War II, 1941-1945 European Theater 57

Conflicts in the Postwar World

Opportunities and Uncertainties, 1957-1975 58

The War in Korea, 1950 59

The Vietnam War, 1957-1975 59

Migration and Immigration

African American Migration, 1940-1970 ... 60

Major Sources of Immigration, 1960s-1990s 61

Involvement in Middle America

United States Involvement in Central America and the Caribbean, 1959-1990 62

Section 8: Entering a New Millennium (1990 & beyond) 63

Our Country Today

The United States 64

Who We Are

African American Population 66

Hispanic Population 66

Asian Population 66

American Indian, Eskimo, and Aleut Population 66

Where We Live

Population 67

Our Way of Life

Income 68

Lifetime Expectance 68

Poverty 69

Unemployment 69

Our Place in the World

World Political 70

Databank

Populations of United States Colonies and States, 1650-1990 72

Facts About the States 74

Index 76

Introducing Atlas of American History

The features of *Atlas of American History* described below enhance understanding of America's past. They support and extend information from textbooks and primary sources. They provide additional links between history and geography.

Features of *Atlas of American History*

▲ Historical Maps

Maps are arranged chronologically. Each map includes a title that describes its content and dates that indicate the period of history it shows. Compare maps of the same area in different time periods to view historical changes.

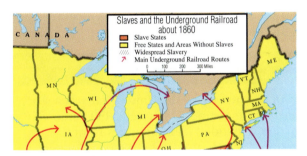

▲ Map Legends and Labels

A map legend explains the colors and symbols used on a map. Historical maps often use solid or dashed lines to indicate routes of explorers or other groups of people. These routes may be labeled on the map. Labels also identify sites of historical events.

Captions

Each map has a caption that helps explain the content of the map. It may provide information about the historical context of the map or point out an important feature of the map. Legends, labels, and captions help tell the story of American history.

◀ Graphs

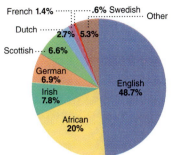

Population by National Origin, 1790

- French 1.4%
- .6% Swedish
- Other
- Dutch 2.7%
- 5.3%
- Scottish 6.6%
- German 6.9%
- Irish 7.8%
- African 20%
- English 48.7%

Some graphs in *Atlas of American History* illustrate information from the maps. Others provide additional information about American history. They may compare data or show changes over time.

Populations of United States Colonies and States, 1650-1990

States	1650	1700	1750	1770
Alabama				
Alaska				
Arizona				
Arkansas				
California				
Colorado				
Connecticut	4,139	25,970	111,280	183,881
Delaware	185	2,470	28,704	35,496

▲ Databank

The databank is a reference section on pages 72-75 of the atlas. It provides tables of information about the United States and its people.

1776

People Juan Bautista de Anza establishes a presidio at San Francisco.

1776

Events Declaration of Independence is signed in Philadelphia.

1776

Literature *"To His Excellency, General Washington,"* by a slave named Phillis Wheatley, is printed in the Pennsylvania Magazine.

◀ Chronologies

Each section of *Atlas of American History* includes a chronology. It lists people, events, and literature associated with the time period represented on the maps in that section. These listings provide connections that aid understanding of history.

I

Idaho, **46**
Illinois, **35a, 37, 41, 42, 43, 46**
Illinois (American Indians), **11**
immigration
  U.S., 1820-1870, **38**
  U.S., 1860-1919, **g45**
  U.S., 1880-1920, **48**
  U.S., 1910, **49**
  U.S., 1960s-1990s, **61**
Inca Empire, South America, **11,**
Inchon, South Korea, **59a**

◀ Index

The index is an alphabetical listing of the places and topics included in *Atlas of American History*. The index shows the page number(s) on which each entry appears. It provides explanatory information about many entries and refers to related entries when appropriate.

Periods of American History

Historians may divide American history into time periods in many different ways. Some periods may center around a theme, such as exploration. Others may center around an important event, such as the American Revolution.

Rand McNally *Atlas of American History* is divided into sections based on time periods described below. Some periods overlap to provide coverage of political and social history. Maps are organized chronologically within each section.

1. Beginnings (prehistory-1620)

Thousands of years ago, hunters from Asia migrated to the lands now called the Americas. These people, now referred to as American Indians or Native Americans, settled throughout the continents. They developed many different cultures, depending upon the environments in which they lived. They remained the only people in the Western Hemisphere until about A.D. 1000, when Vikings from Norway migrated to the coast of North America.

During the 1400s, European demand for Asian goods led Columbus to sail west across the Atlantic Ocean in search of a route to Asia. His discovery of a world previously unknown to Europeans touched off an age of exploration. During the 1500s, Europeans explored and claimed land in the Americas.

2. Establishing Colonies (1600-1775)

During the 1600s and early 1700s, Europeans came to the Americas for many different reasons. English settlers came seeking the freedom to worship as they pleased. Spaniards came to find gold and to spread Christianity. French trappers came to establish fur trade. Dutch settlers came for the promise of land. In addition, many Africans were brought to the Americas as slaves.

By the mid-1700s, English claims extended along the Atlantic coast, and the French controlled the vast interior of North America. Britain and France competed for control of the continent. As a result of the French and Indian War (1754-1763), Britain gained Canada and all of North America east of the Mississippi River.

3. Forming a New Nation (1775-1800)

English settlers in North America developed a prosperous economy and a way of life that differed from that in Great Britain. They began to resent Britain's control. They declared their independence and fought a revolution to win their freedom. As a result, the United States became an independent nation.

The original thirteen states stretched along the Atlantic coast. The western boundary of the new nation extended to the Mississippi River. Americans began to settle lands west of the Appalachian Mountains. The national government passed laws providing for the sale of western lands and the addition of new states.

4. The Nation Expands and Changes (1790-1870)

Much of the history of the United States is a story of westward movement. Between 1803 and 1848, the nation expanded its boundaries from the Mississippi River to the Pacific Coast. Pioneers had settled most of the land east of the Mississippi River by 1840.

People	**1769** Junípero Serra starts first Spanish mission in what is now California.	**1804** Meriwether Lewis and William Clark lead expedition from St. Louis to the Pacific Ocean.	**1933** President Franklin Roosevelt creates TVA to develop the natural resources of the Tennessee Valle
Events	**about 700 B.C.** The Adena (early North American Indians) build mounds in what is now Ohio.	**1565** Spaniards establish St. Augustine, FL, first permanent European settlement in what is now the United States.	**1787** Founders write the U.S. Constitution in Philadelphia, PA.
Literature	**1608** *A True Relation of Occurrences in Virginia*, by John Smith, describes the founding of Jamestown.	**1704** Sarah Kemble Knight's *Journal* describes the author's horseback journey from Boston to New York.	**1868** *Little Women*, by Louisa May Alcott, tells the story of four sisters growing up in New England in the mid-1800s.

In the early 1800s, fur trappers, traders, and miners pushed west of the Mississippi River, seeking economic opportunities. Soon they were followed by farmers and ranchers who settled the land. The promise of land and the hope of a better life also attracted millions of European immigrants to the United States.

5. A Nation Divided (1850-1865)

Different ways of life developed in the North and the South. Southern agriculture was based on slave labor. Industrial states in the North outlawed slavery. As settlers moved westward, new states were created. The question of whether to allow slavery in the new states led to conflict between the North and the South.

Debate and compromise failed to solve the problems. Eleven southern states withdrew from the Union. Between 1861 and 1865, the North and the South fought against each other in the Civil War.

6. Emerging as a Modern Nation (1860-1920)

Within 25 years after the Civil War ended, the process of settling the United States from coast to coast was completed. The settlement of the West also brought an end to the Native American way of life. The federal government sent soldiers to stop uprisings and move Indians onto reservations.

As the United States became an industrial nation, people moved to cities to work in factories. Millions of European immigrants also came to the United States seeking jobs.

The nation acquired territories overseas and began to emerge as a modern nation. By fighting in World War I, the United States also proved that it had become a world power.

7. Challenges and Changes in the 20th Century (1920-1990)

A period of prosperity followed World War I. However, the stock market crash in 1929 plunged the nation into an economic depression that lasted throughout the 1930s. During those years, the actions of powerful dictators in Europe led to World War II.

The United States fought in World War II from 1941 to 1945. It emerged as the leader of the free world, and the Soviet Union emerged as the leader of the Communist world. During the following decades, the United States intervened in many parts of the world to stop the spread of Communism.

8. Entering a New Millennium (1990 and beyond)

The United States has compiled information about the American population every ten years since 1790, when the first census was taken. According to the 1990 census, more than three-fourths of the country's 250 million people lived in cities. Americans born in 1990 could expect to live longer than any previous generation. Although many Americans lived in poverty in 1990, the United States had one of the world's highest standards of living.

The United States faces many challenges as it enters a new millennium. It must meet the needs of its diverse population. It must also continue its role of leadership in a rapidly changing world. The story of America is ongoing because today's events will become tomorrow's history.

1955	1969	1989
Rosa Parks protests segregation in Montgomery, AL by refusing to give up bus seat to white passenger.	U.S. astronaut Neil Armstrong becomes first person to walk on the moon.	Colin Powell, son of Jamaican immigrants, becomes first African American to head Joint Chiefs of Staff.

1848	1941	1970
Discovery of gold in California brings settlers to the West.	Japanese bombing of Pearl Harbor, Hawaii, brings U.S. into World War II.	Americans participate in Earth Day, a nationwide demonstration of concern for the environment.

1932	1976	1989
Little House in the Big Woods, by Laura Ingalls Wilder, describes life in the Midwest in the 1870s and 1880s.	*Roots: The Saga of an American Family*, by Alex Haley, traces the author's ancestry back to the African slave trade.	*The Joy Luck Club*, by Amy Tan, tells the experiences of Chinese women in San Francisco after World War II.

Benefits of Using Rand McNally *Atlas of American History*

Events gain fuller meaning.

Knowing where events took place gives them fuller meaning and often explains causes and effects. For example, the map of the final campaign of the American Revolution, on page 27, shows how American and French forces trapped the British at Yorktown. It helps explain why Cornwallis surrendered.

Connections among events are clarified.

Through the visual power of historical maps, the links between and among events become clear. The maps on pages 12 and 13 show international trade routes, 1350-1450, and Portuguese routes to India in the 1400s. They help explain why Europeans wanted to find an all-water route to Asia. They provide the background to understanding the age of exploration that followed Columbus's discovery of the Americas.

Similarities and differences become apparent.

The maps in *Atlas of American History* provide an opportunity to compare and contrast places over time. Compare the map of North America in 1763, on page 23, with the map of North America in 1783 on page 28. These maps show the emergence of the United States on a continent claimed by Britain and Spain.

The maps in this atlas also provide an opportunity to compare and contrast regions of the United States. The map titled "A Quarreling People," on page 41, indicates differences between the North and the South at the time of the Civil War.

The influence of sense of place is conveyed.

Maps in *Atlas of American History* convey people's sense of place at a particular time in history. The map titled "Opportunities and Uncertainties," on page 58, is a good example. The map's polar projection emphasizes how near the Soviet Union is to the United States. It reflects Americans' fear of nuclear attack from the north during the postwar period of tension between the United States and the Soviet Union.

Trends emerge.

The maps in this atlas show trends in American history. The map of Westward Expansion, on pages 36-37, shows the sequence in which the United States acquired land. It indicates the westward movement of settlement patterns. The maps on pages 38, 48, and 61 indicate changing trends in immigration.

The story of American history is communicated.

The text in *Atlas of American History* presents a chronological overview of American history and summarizes key events. It provides cross curricular connections by listing literature that clarifies or expands historical understandings. It highlights people whose accomplishments reflect American ideals.

The *Did You Know?* feature on each section opening page provides an interesting sidelight to history. Like the example below, each of these features demonstrates how history has influenced the American experience.

A picture of the Greek god Atlas, supporting the earth on his shoulders, appeared on the title page of an early book of maps. Later, people began to call a collection of maps an *atlas*.

Section 1 (Prehistory-1620)

Beginnings

To learn about **prehistory**, or the time before human beings learned to write, scientists study the physical evidence that early people left behind. This evidence suggests the first Americans migrated from Asia between 25,000 and 8,000 years ago. The descendants of these people, now called Native Americans or American Indians, spread throughout the Americas and developed different cultures.

◄ The Cliff Palace in Mesa Verde, Colorado, was built by the Anasazi around 1100.

Historical evidence indicates that Vikings from Norway established a settlement in North America about A.D. 1000. During the 1400s, increased demand for Asian goods led European nations to seek a water route to Asia. Columbus was attempting to achieve this goal when he discovered a world previously unknown to Europeans.

In 1524 Verrazano ► explored the Atlantic coast of what is now North Carolina.

During the 1500s, European explorers who came to the Americas found continents inhabited by native peoples of diverse cultures, from hunters and gatherers to advanced civilizations. Although figures vary greatly, the graph at the right indicates estimates of Native American populations around that time.

Did You Know ?

Scientists discovered a spearhead among bones of ancient bison near Folsom, New Mexico. These animals became extinct about 10,000 years ago. This discovery proved people had migrated to the region by about 8000 B.C.

Estimates of Native American Populations in 1492

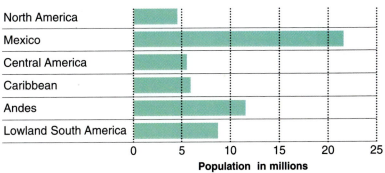

Region	Population in millions
North America	~4.5
Mexico	~21.5
Central America	~5.5
Caribbean	~6
Andes	~11.5
Lowland South America	~8.5

(scale: 0 5 10 15 20 25 — Population in millions)

People

about A.D. 1000
Leif Ericson establishes a Viking settlement on the east coast of North America.

1492
Christopher Columbus lands on San Salvador.

1587
Virginia Dare, first English child born in America, is born on Roanoke Island.

Events

about 23,000 B.C.
First Americans probably migrate from Asia to North America.

1325
Aztecs build Tenochtitlán on site of present-day Mexico City.

about 1570
Five Indian tribes in what is now New York form League of the Iroquois.

Literature

1298
Description of the World, by Marco Polo, tells of the Italian trader's journey from Venice to China.

1504
New World, a letter by Amerigo Vespucci, becomes the basis for naming America.

1552
In Defense of the Indian, by Bartolomé de Las Casas, criticizes the Spanish for abusing Indians on Hispaniola.

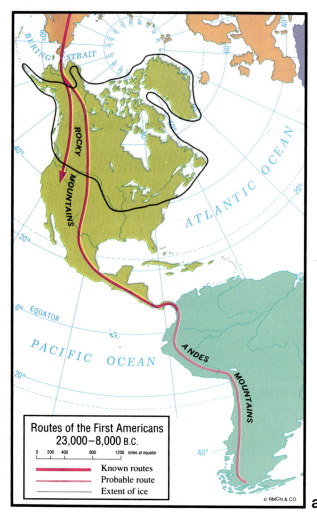

◀ During the Ice Ages, much of Earth's water was frozen in glaciers. These huge ice sheets covered much of what is now Canada and the northern United States. Scientists believe a land bridge existed where the Bering Strait now separates Asia and Alaska. Between 25,000 and 10,000 years ago, people from Asia may have migrated across the land bridge and spread throughout North America and South America.

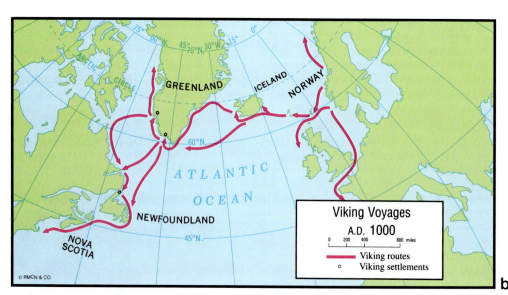

▲ About A.D. 1000, Norwegian Vikings, who had settled in Greenland, explored the coast of North America. They established a settlement in what is now Newfoundland, Canada.

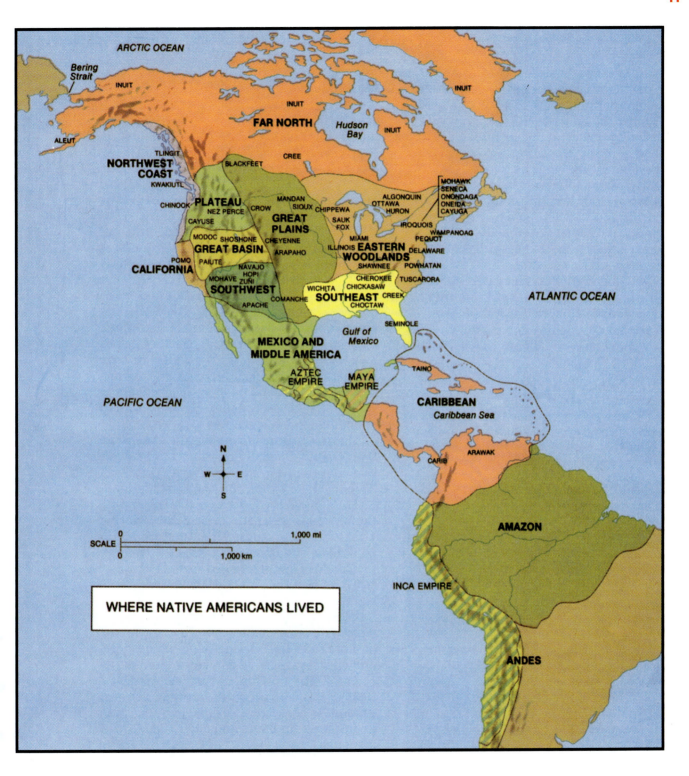

WHERE NATIVE AMERICANS LIVED

▲ Environments in which tribes of Native Americans or American Indians followed a similar way of life are called culture areas. The culture areas shown on the map existed around 1500, when Europeans began to arrive in the Americas. The map also lists major tribes of Native Americans within each culture area.

amber
flax
fur
hemp
honey
slaves
tallow
timber
wax
whalebone

copper
iron
tallow
timber

North Sea

iron
copper
lead
silver
wine
textiles
coal

coal
textiles
tin

Novgorod

Tver
Moscow

Kazan

gold
iron
prec
hors
carp
man

Lubeck

London

Antwerp

Paris

Kiev

Lemberg
(Lwow)

Azov
(Tana)

Saray

Astrakhan

ATLANTIC OCEAN

Venice

Genoa

Marseilles

Barcelona

CORSICA

Adriatic Sea

Ragusa

Moncastro

Kaffa

Black Sea

Istanbul
(Constantinople)

Salonika

Bursa

Trabzon

Darband
silk

Tabriz

silk

Caspian Sea

mercury
sugar
wine
wool

SARDINIA

Naples

Lisbon
Seville

Granada

Palermo
SICILY

Algiers
Tunis

Mediterranean Sea

CRETE

Famagusta
CYPRUS

Ayas

Beirut

Aleppo

Damascus

Acre

Isfa

Fez
Qran

copper iron

Tripoli

Barqa

Alexandria

Cairo

Qulzum

Baghdad

Basra

Persian Gu

animals
carpets
copper
iron
manufactures
naphtha
paper
textiles

Matrakesh

Agadir

Ghadames
cotton
gold
ivory
salt
slaves

Marzuq

Ghat

Taghaza

Agadès

Bilma

Aydhab

Jidda
Mecca

Sana'

Shihr

Arawan
Timbuktu
Gao

El Fasher

Sennar

Sawakin

Aden

Zeila

Gulf of Aden

Berbera

Sokoto
Kano

Mogadishu

Equator

Malindi
Mombasa

ZANZIBAR

gold
ivory
precious wood
slaves

Kilwa

Mozambique

Quelimane

MADAGASCAR

Sofala

INTERNATIONAL TRADE
1350–1450

——— Major Sea Routes

——— Major Land Routes

○ Beijing Principal Trade Centers

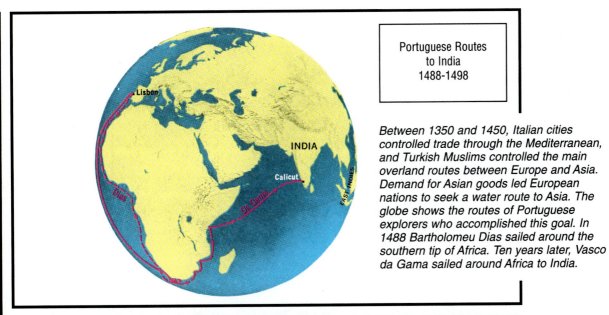

Portuguese Routes to India 1488-1498

Between 1350 and 1450, Italian cities controlled trade through the Mediterranean, and Turkish Muslims controlled the main overland routes between Europe and Asia. Demand for Asian goods led European nations to seek a water route to Asia. The globe shows the routes of Portuguese explorers who accomplished this goal. In 1488 Bartholomeu Dias sailed around the southern tip of Africa. Ten years later, Vasco da Gama sailed around Africa to India.

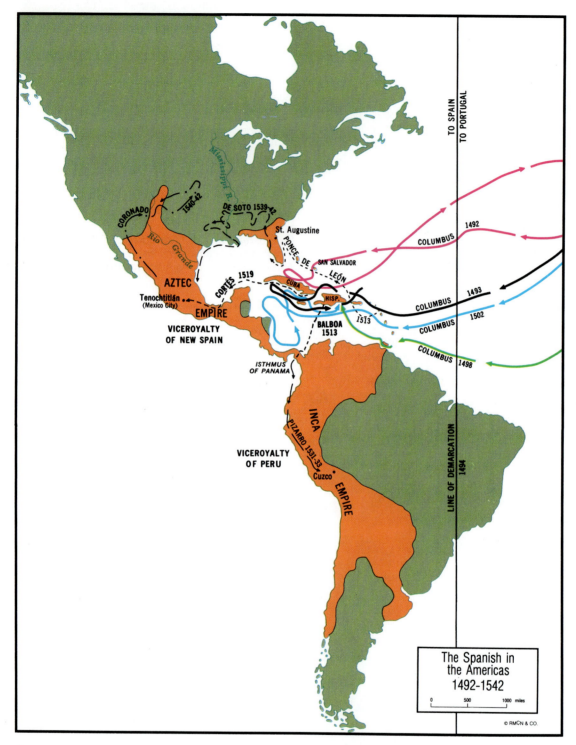

The Spanish in
the Americas
1492-1542

0   500   1000 miles

© RMCN & CO.

▲ The voyages of Christopher Columbus led other Europeans to explore the Americas.
Pope Alexander VI established the Line of Demarcation to prevent disputes between
Spain and Portugal over lands their explorers claimed. The Spanish conquered
Indian empires in Mexico and Peru.

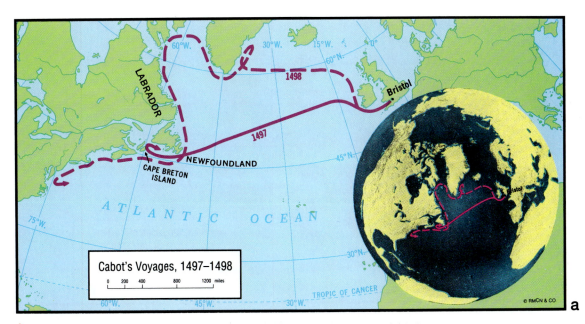

▲ John Cabot attempted to reach Asia by a northwest route across the Atlantic Ocean. In 1497 and 1498, Cabot explored the coasts of present-day Labrador, Newfoundland, and Cape Breton Island (Nova Scotia). His voyages gave England a claim to North America.

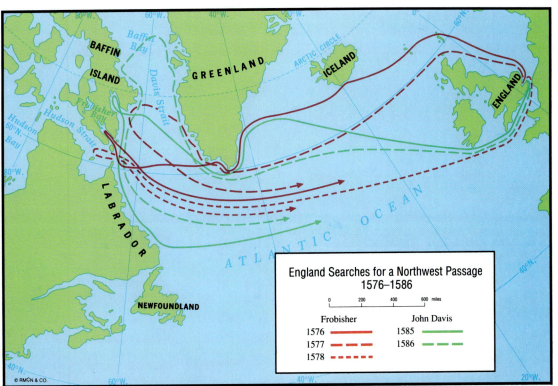

▲ In the 1570s and 1580s, England renewed its search for a water route to Asia through North America. Martin Frobisher and John Davis explored the Atlantic coast of what is now Canada and the area between Greenland and Baffin Island.

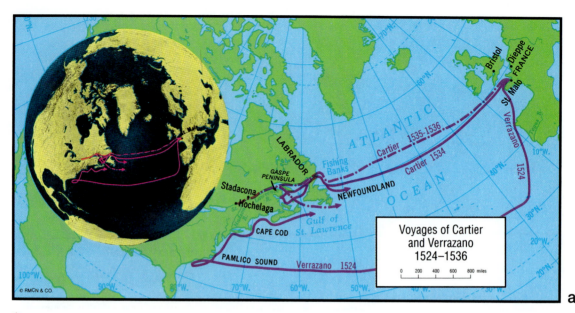

Voyages of Cartier and Verrazano 1524–1536

▲ France also sent explorers in search of a water route through North America. Giovanni da Verrazano explored the Atlantic coast from what is now North Carolina to Newfoundland. Jacques Cartier explored the St. Lawrence River and claimed the region for France.

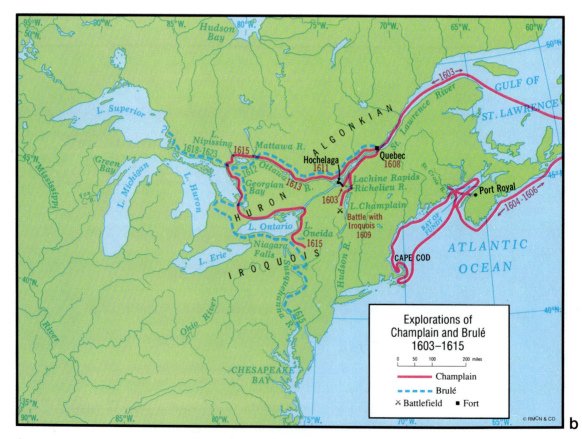

Explorations of Champlain and Brulé 1603–1615

▲ Samuel de Champlain extended French claims in North America. In 1608 he founded the city of Quebec. He then helped the Algonquin and Huron Indians defeat the Iroquois. Etienne Brulé lived among the Huron Indians and explored the river systems of northeastern North America for France.

Establishing Colonies

Between 1600 and 1775, Europeans established **colonies**, or settlements ruled by their homelands, in North America. The English settled along the Atlantic coast and eventually took over Dutch and Swedish colonies established there. By 1732 thirteen English colonies stretched along the east coast of the present United States from New Hampshire to Georgia.

The French claimed the vast interior of North America. English attempts to settle west of the Appalachians led to conflict between France and Britain. The French and Indian War gave Britain control of all land east of the Mississippi River.

The colonial population grew rapidly due to a high birth rate and increased immigration. People came to America seeking religious freedom and economic opportunities. Slave traders also brought thousands of unwilling immigrants from Africa.

◄ This stone canopy stands near the Massachusetts shore. It covers Plymouth Rock, which marks the spot near which the Pilgrims are believed to have stepped ashore.

Reproductions of ships that brought the first settlers to Jamestown are on the James River in Virginia. They are near the site of the first permanent English settlement in America. ►

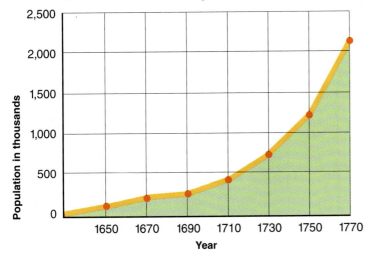

Growth of Colonial Population

Graph: Population in thousands (y-axis, 0 to 2,500) vs. Year (x-axis, 1650 to 1770)

Did You Know ?

Swedish settlers introduced log cabins in America. They built these houses along the Delaware River in the 1640s.

People

1614	1626	1682
Pocahontas, daughter of Chief Powhatan, marries Jamestown colonist John Rolfe.	Peter Minuit purchases Manhattan Island from local Indians.	LaSalle claims Mississippi River Valley for France.

Events

1607	1620	1754
Jamestown is founded.	Pilgrims settle Plymouth Colony.	French and Indian War begins at Fort Necessity.

Literature

1640	1650	1733
The *Bay Psalm Book* is the first book written and published in the American colonies.	*The Tenth Muse Lately Sprung Up in America*, by Anne Bradstreet, describes home life in colonial New England.	*Poor Richard's Almanac*, by Ben Franklin, is published in Philadelphia.

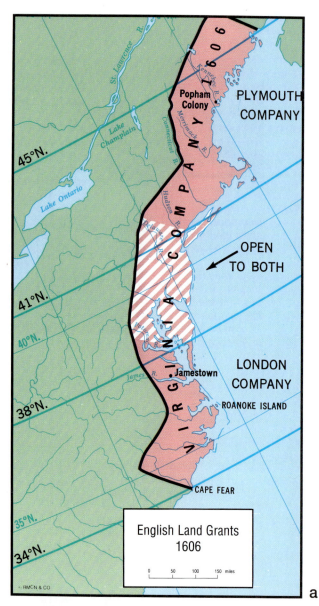

English Land Grants 1606

Popham Colony
PLYMOUTH COMPANY

45°N.

St. Lawrence R.
Kennebec R.
Merrimack R.
Connecticut R.
Lake Champlain
Lake Ontario
Hudson R.
Delaware R.

OPEN TO BOTH

41°N.

40°N.

V I R G I N I A   C O M P A N Y   1606

Potomac R.

James R.
Jamestown

LONDON COMPANY

ROANOKE ISLAND

38°N.

35°N.

34°N.

CAPE FEAR

English Land Grants 1606

0   50   100   150 miles

RMCN & CO.

a

▲ The Plymouth Company and the London Company were groups of stockholders within the Virginia Company. Each group obtained a land grant from the English king to establish a colony in America. Land between 38° and 41° north latitude was open to both groups. Neither group was allowed to settle within 100 miles of the other.

The Dutch bought Manhattan Island from Native Americans and established a fortified trading center called New Amsterdam. They established other settlements along the Hudson River and later took over Swedish settlements along the Delaware River.

▼

Ft. Orange (Albany) (1623)
RENSSELAERSWYCK
ENGLISH TERRITORY
CATSKILL MTS.
Hudson River
Long Island Sound
MANHATTAN ISLAND
New Amsterdam (New York) (1624)
Susquehanna R.
Delaware R.
Schuylkill R.
Ft. Nassau (Dutch) (1623)
Ft. Christina (Wilmington) (1638)
New Gothenburg (1643)
Ft. Casimir (Dutch)
Delaware Bay
Swaanendael (Lewes) (1631)
ENGLISH TERRITORY
Chesapeake Bay
ATLANTIC OCEAN

Hackensack R.
Hudson River
MANHATTAN I.
East R.
New Amsterdam
STATEN I.
Breuckelen
New Utrecht

Dutch and Swedish Settlements 1623–1643

0   25   50   75 miles

▪ Dutch   ○ Swedish

RMCN & CO.

b

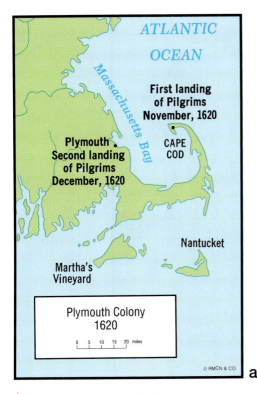

▲ The Pilgrims named their colony Plymouth, after the English port from which they had sailed.

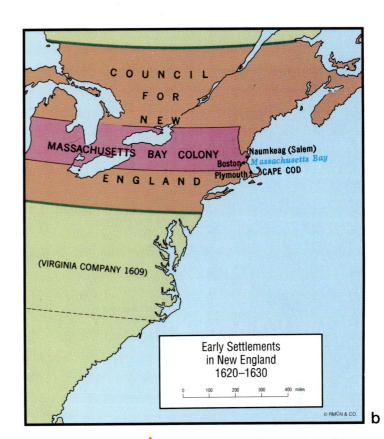

▲ In 1620 a group called the Council for New England received a land grant from the English king. The Massachusetts Bay Colony was established on this land in 1628.

◀ The Puritans established settlements in the eastern part of Massachusetts, shown in blue on the map. Plymouth became part of the Massachusetts Colony. People who disagreed with Puritan views left Massachusetts and established new colonies.

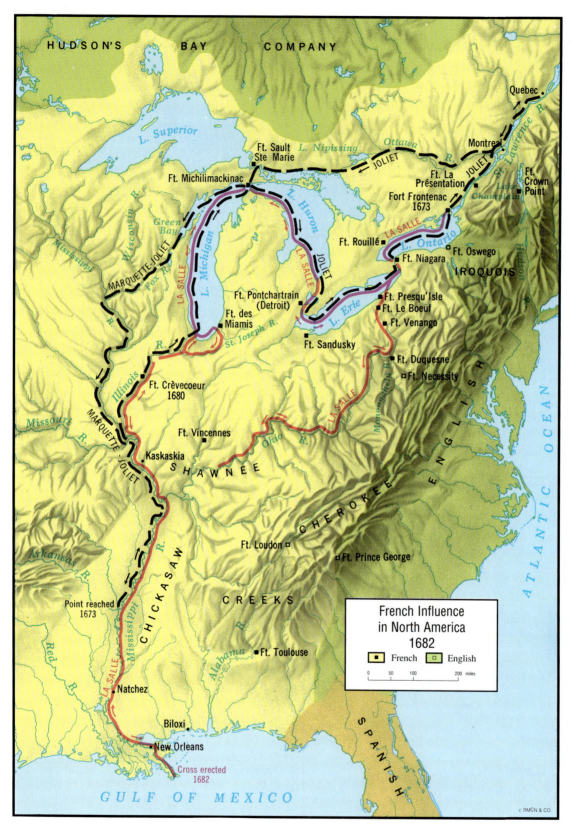

French Influence in North America 1682

■ French   ▢ English

0   50   100   200 miles

▲ France claimed the vast interior of North America, but it had little control over the region because of a lack of settlers.

The Thirteen Original
British Colonies, 1750

0   200   400 Miles

Copyright by Rand McNally & Company. Made in U.S.A.

▲ *In about 150 years, the British established the 13 colonies that would become the
United States. By 1750 the British colonies had a population of more than 1 million.*

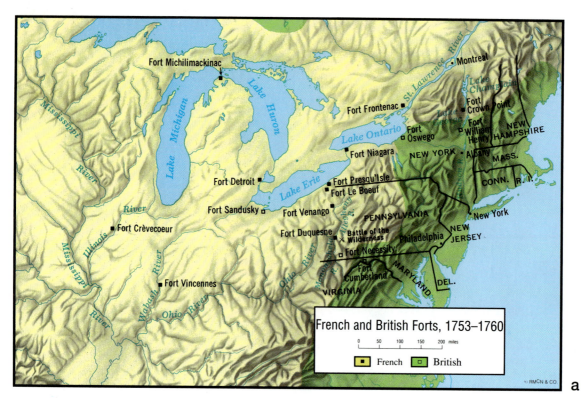

▲ To keep the British east of the Appalachians, the French built a string of forts from Lake Erie to the Ohio River.

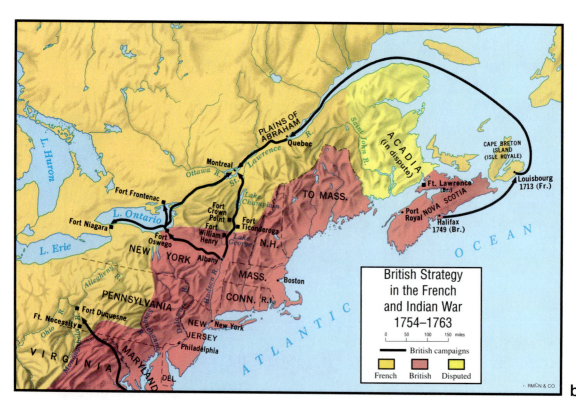

▲ The British captured French forts in the St. Lawrence Valley and the eastern Great Lakes region.

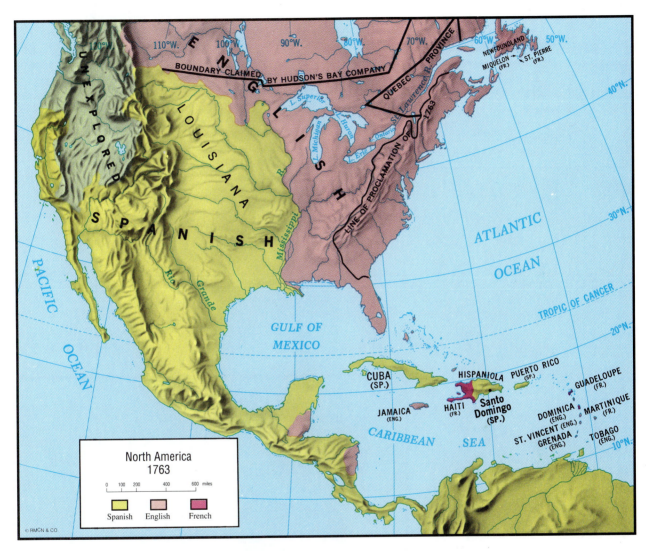

The French and Indian War ended French control in North America. According
to the Treaty of Paris in 1763, France kept only a few islands in the Caribbean.
Britain acquired Canada and all French lands east of the Mississippi River.
From Spain, France's ally in the war, Britain acquired Florida. To make up for
the loss of Florida, France gave Spain the vast land between the Mississippi
River and the Rocky Mountains.

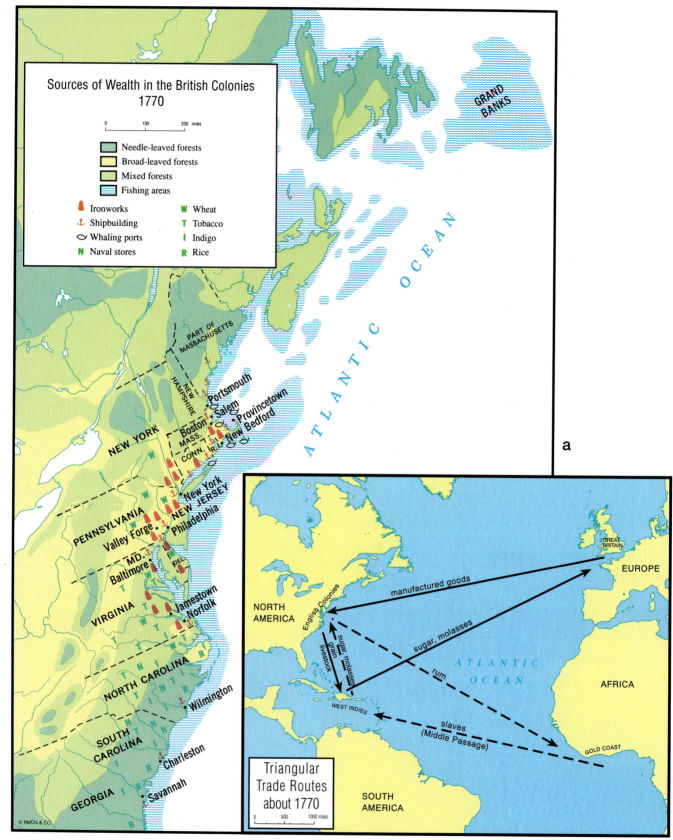

Sources of Wealth in the British Colonies 1770

0   100   200 miles

- Needle-leaved forests
- Broad-leaved forests
- Mixed forests
- Fishing areas

- Ironworks
- Shipbuilding
- Whaling ports
- **N** Naval stores
- **W** Wheat
- **T** Tobacco
- **I** Indigo
- **R** Rice

GRAND BANKS

ATLANTIC OCEAN

PART OF MASSACHUSETTS

NEW HAMPSHIRE

Portsmouth
Salem
Provincetown
Boston
MASS.
New Bedford
CONN. R.I.

NEW YORK

New York
NEW JERSEY
Philadelphia

PENNSYLVANIA
Valley Forge

MD.
Baltimore
DEL.

VIRGINIA
Jamestown
Norfolk

NORTH CAROLINA
Wilmington

SOUTH CAROLINA
Charleston

GEORGIA
Savannah

© RMCN & CO.

a

Triangular Trade Routes about 1770

0   500   1000 miles

NORTH AMERICA

English Colonies

GREAT BRITAIN

EUROPE

manufactured goods

sugar, molasses

rum

sugar, molasses
grain
livestock

WEST INDIES

AFRICA

slaves (Middle Passage)

GOLD COAST

ATLANTIC OCEAN

SOUTH AMERICA

b

▲ *Some colonial trade involved the exchange of goods for slaves. Thousands of unwilling immigrants from Africa suffered terribly during the voyage to America.*

Forming a New Nation

Between 1775 and 1800, the United States became an independent nation and established a new government. The Revolutionary War began when American minutemen clashed with British soldiers at Lexington and Concord in 1775. It ended in 1781 when Washington's troops, aided by French forces, defeated Cornwallis and his British troops at Yorktown.

The Treaty of Paris of 1783 recognized the independence of the United States and established its borders. The nation extended from the Atlantic Coast to the Mississippi River. The new states **ceded**, or gave up, their western lands to the federal government. The government created the Northwest Territory and provided for the sale of land to settlers.

The Constitution, ratified in 1788, established the government that remains in effect today. The census in 1790 indicated the national origins of the American population.

◄ This statue in Boston honors Paul Revere's historic ride on April 18, 1775. Revere rode from Boston to Lexington to warn colonists that the British were coming.

During the 1700s, Spaniards built missions, like the one shown here, throughout the southwestern part of the present United States. ▶

Population by National Origin, 1790

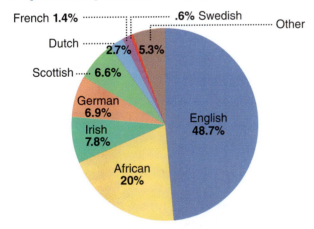

French **1.4%** · **.6%** Swedish
Dutch · · · · · · · · · · · · · · · · · Other
2.7% **5.3%**
Scottish · · · · · **6.6%**
German **6.9%**
Irish **7.8%**
English **48.7%**
African **20%**

Did You Know ?

The states carved from the Northwest Territory might be different if Thomas Jefferson had named them. He suggested such names as Dolypotamia, Assinisippia, and Metropotamia.

People

1776	1789	1791
Juan Bautista de Anza establishes a presidio at San Francisco.	George Washington takes presidential oath of office in New York.	Benjamin Banneker, an African American surveyor, helps plan Washington, D.C.

Events

1776	1785	1800
Declaration of Independence is signed in Philadelphia.	Land Ordinance provides plan for sale of land in the Northwest Territory.	Washington, D.C. becomes the national capital.

Literature

1776	1782	1787
"To His Excellency, General Washington," by a slave named Phillis Wheatley, is printed in the Pennsylvania Magazine.	*Letters from an American Farmer,* by Jean de Crèvecoeur, describes social customs in the United States.	*The Federalist,* by Hamilton, Madison, and Jay, urges New York to ratify the Constitution.

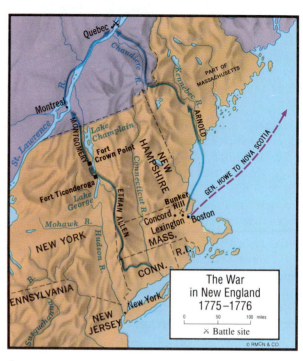

▲ On the way to Concord, the British were met at Lexington by minutemen who had been warned by William Dawes and Paul Revere.

▲ Americans captured British artillery at Forts Ticonderoga and Crown Point. They used the cannons in Boston, where they forced General William Howe and his troops to leave. An American invasion of Canada, led by General Richard Montgomery and Benedict Arnold, failed.

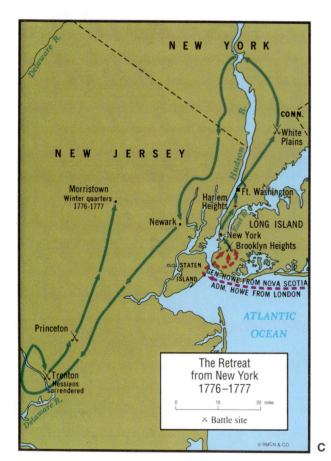

▲ The British victory on Long Island forced George Washington and his troops to retreat from New York. After victories at Trenton and Princeton, American troops moved to winter quarters at Morristown.

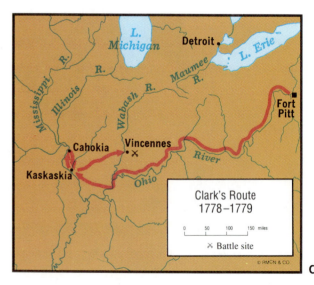

▲ Troops led by George Rogers Clark captured British settlements in the Ohio Valley.

Northern Campaigns
1777

0   25   50   75 miles

British   American

✕ Battle site

© RMcN & CO.

a

▲ Americans suffered heavy losses at
Philadelphia and Germantown, but their
victory at Saratoga convinced France to
enter the war on the American side.

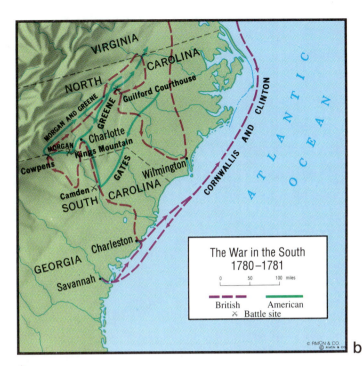

The War in the South
1780–1781

0   50   100 miles

British   American
✕ Battle site

© RMcN & CO.

b

▲ British troops sailed to major ports in the South.

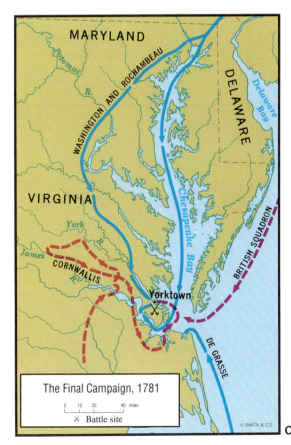

The Final Campaign, 1781

0   10   20   40 miles

✕ Battle site

© RMcN & CO.

c

▲ The war ended at Yorktown when
General Charles Cornwallis and his
troops surrendered.

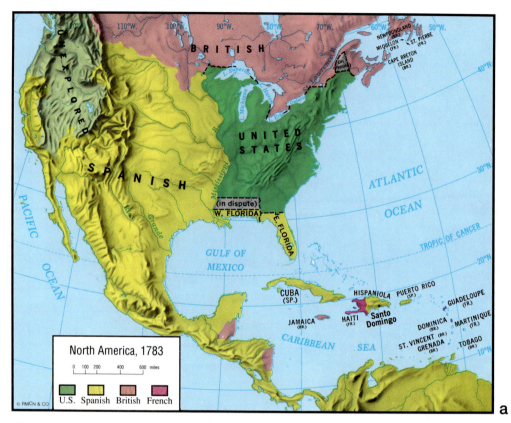

▲ *The Treaty of Paris of 1783 established the boundaries of the United States. The new nation extended from the Atlantic Ocean to the Mississippi River and from 31° north latitude to the Canadian border. The treaty granted Florida to Spain.*

▲ *Spaniards established forts to protect their lands and missions to spread their faith.*

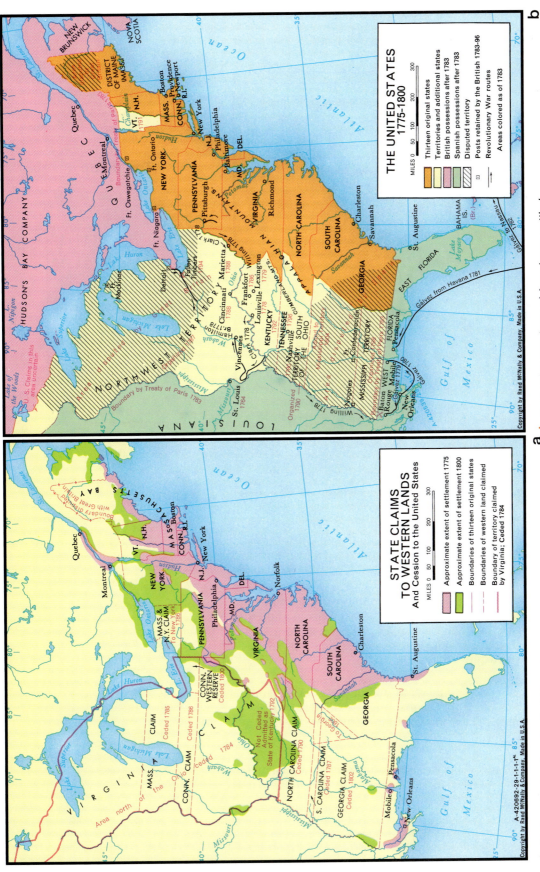

b

THE UNITED STATES 1775–1800

MILES 0 50 100 200 300

- Thirteen original states
- Territories and additional states
- British possessions after 1783
- Spanish possessions after 1783
- Disputed territory
- ⊡ Posts retained by the British 1783–96
- Revolutionary War routes
- Areas colored as of 1783

Copyright by Rand McNally & Company. Made in U.S.A.

▲ **a** Increasing numbers of Americans settled
west of the Appalachians. Kentucky and
Tennessee became states. Britain and
Spain disputed areas of land added to the
United States in 1783.

STATE CLAIMS TO WESTERN LANDS
And Cession to the United States

MILES 0 50 100 200 300

- Approximate extent of settlement 1775
- Approximate extent of settlement 1800
- Boundaries of thirteen original states
- Boundaries of western land claimed
- Boundary of territory claimed
  by Virginia; Ceded 1784

A-420692-29-1-1-1ᴬ
Copyright by Rand McNally & Company. Made in U.S.A.

▲ States with western land claims were
asked to put the good of the country
above their own interests. Virginia was
first to give up its claims. By 1802 all
states had ceded their western lands to
the United States.

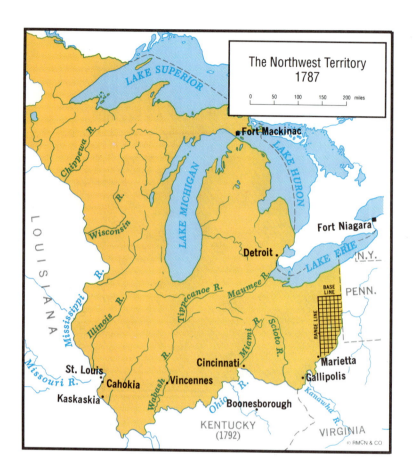

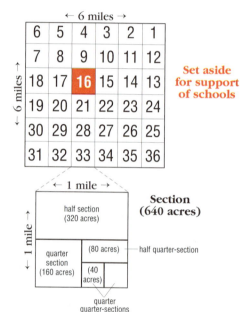

The Northwest Territory was land north of the Ohio River that later became the states of Ohio, Indiana, Illinois, Michigan, and Wisconsin. The Land Ordinance of 1785 provided a plan for the sale of this land.

Public lands were divided into townships that were six miles square. Each township was divided into 36 sections, as shown on the diagram. Each section consisted of 640 acres, and it sold for $1 per acre. The small white square in the grid on the map represents one township.

In the 1780s, few settlers could afford to buy a section of land. Companies such as the Ohio Company and Scioto Company bought land from the government and divided it into smaller lots. Then they sold it to settlers at a profit.

Section 16 in each township was set aside by the government for the support of education. Settlers could rent or sell this land to raise money for public schools.

Section 4 (1790-1870)

The Nation Expands & Changes

Between 1790 and 1870, the United States expanded its boundaries to the Pacific Coast. Through the Louisiana Purchase in 1803, it acquired the vast land between the Mississippi River and the Rocky Mountains. Through war with Mexico, 1846-1848, it gained land in the Southwest. Through a treaty with Britain in 1846, it gained land in the Pacific Northwest. Within 70 years after the United States became an independent nation, it had tripled in size.

Explorers, trappers, and traders blazed trails to the West. Pioneers rapidly settled new territories, pushing the **frontier**, or edge of settled land, west of the Mississippi River. Settlers followed the Oregon Trail to the Pacific Northwest. Mormons traveled to Utah in search of religious freedom. Gold seekers poured into California. Millions of immigrants from Europe came to the United States seeking a better life.

The Gateway Arch stands along the Mississippi River in St. Louis. It honors the Louisiana Purchase and the pioneers who settled the West.

This monument marks the Oregon Trail, which thousands of pioneers traveled from Independence, Missouri, to the Oregon country.

Did You Know?

Francis Scott Key wrote "The Star-Spangled Banner" during the War of 1812 as he watched the bombardment of Fort McHenry from a ship in Baltimore Harbor. The words were set to music and later became our national anthem.

Area of Selected Lands Added to the United States, 1803-1867

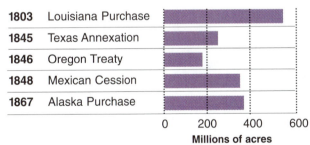

1803	Louisiana Purchase
1845	Texas Annexation
1846	Oregon Treaty
1848	Mexican Cession
1867	Alaska Purchase

Millions of acres

People

1803 President Thomas Jefferson purchases Louisiana Territory from France.

1847 Brigham Young leads Mormon migration from Illinois to the Great Salt Lake.

1848 Elizabeth Cady Stanton and Lucretia Mott hold women's rights convention in New York.

Events

1819 United States acquires Florida from Spain.

1825 Erie Canal links the Great Lakes and Atlantic Ocean.

1849 Gold rush brings thousands of people to California.

Literature

1820 "Rip Van Winkle," by Washington Irving, is set in the Catskill Mountains.

1827 *The Prairie*, by James Fenimore Cooper, describes frontier life on the western plains.

1854 *Walden*, by Henry David Thoreau, describes the beauty of nature in Massachusetts.

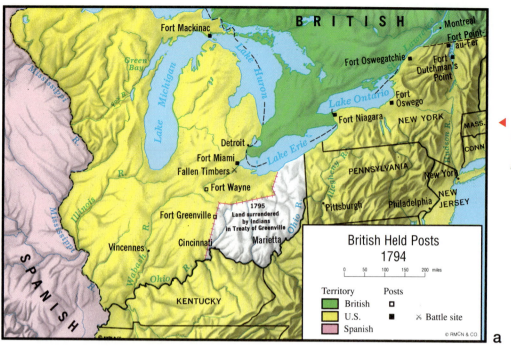

◀ *The British violated the Treaty of Paris of 1783 by keeping posts in U.S. territory.*

B R I T I S H

Fort Mackinac

Green Bay

Lake Michigan

Lake Huron

Montreal

Fort Point-au-Fer

Fort Oswegatchie

Fort Dutchman's Point

Lake Ontario

Fort Oswego

Fort Niagara

NEW YORK

MASS.

CONN.

Detroit

Lake Erie

Fort Miami

Fallen Timbers ✕

Fort Wayne

New York

PENNSYLVANIA

Allegheny R.

Hudson R.

NEW JERSEY

Fort Greenville

1795 Land surrendered by Indians in Treaty of Greenville

Pittsburgh

Philadelphia

Vincennes

Cincinnati

Marietta

Ohio R.

Wabash R.

Illinois R.

Mississippi R.

S P A N I S H

KENTUCKY

British Held Posts 1794

0   50   100   150   200 miles

Territory	Posts
British (green)	□
U.S. (yellow)	■
Spanish (pink)	✕ Battle site

© RMCN & CO.

a

Ft. Clatsop

Columbia R.

B R I T I S H

LAKE SUPERIOR

Great Falls

LEWIS

Yellowstone R.

CLARK

Ft. Mandan

M A N D A N

L O U I S I A N A

OREGON COUNTRY (Claimed by British)

ROCKY MOUNTAINS

SHOSHONE

Snake R.

GREAT SALT LAKE

Missouri R.

LAKE MICHIGAN

San Francisco

Platte R.

PAWNEE

Osage R.

St. Louis

PIKE'S PEAK

Colorado R.

Los Angeles

Santa Fe

P U R C H A S E

Arkansas R.

Mississippi R.

San Diego

S P A N I S H

Red R.

New Orleans

Rio Grande

Louisiana Purchase, 1803, and Its Exploration, 1804–1807

0   100   200   300   400   500 miles

— Lewis and Clark—Going 1804–1805
--- Lewis and Clark—Returning 1806
— Zebulon Pike—1806–1807

© RMCN & CO.

b

▲ *Explorations of the Louisiana Purchase by Lewis and Clark and Pike provided valuable information about lands west of the Mississippi River.*

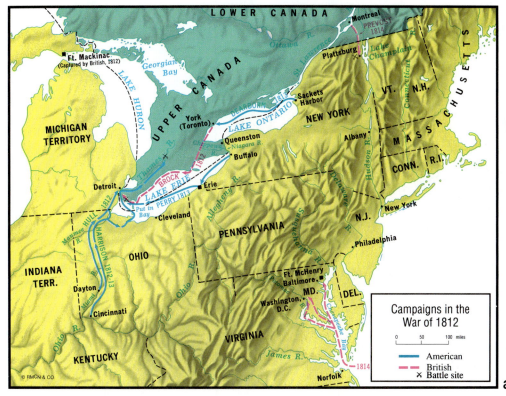

◀ *Campaigns in the War of 1812 were widely scattered. They included a decisive U.S. victory on Lake Erie as well as the British capture and burning of Washington, D.C.*

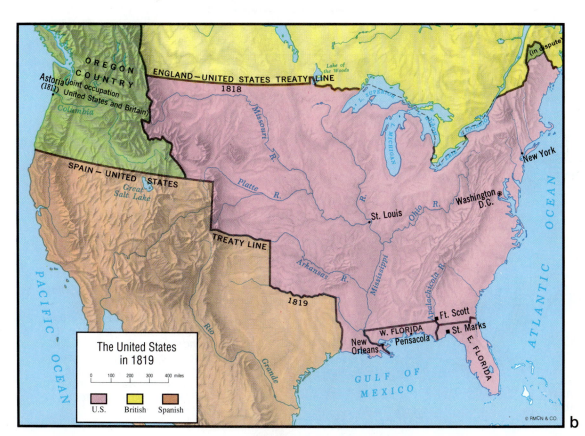

▲ *The Treaty of Ghent set a boundary between U.S. and British lands and allowed both nations to settle the Oregon Country. The Adams-Onís Treaty set a boundary between U.S. and Spanish lands and gave Florida to the United States.*

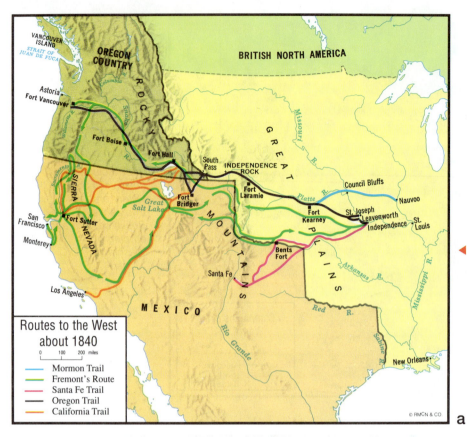

Routes to the West about 1840

0   100   200 miles

— Mormon Trail
— Fremont's Route
— Santa Fe Trail
— Oregon Trail
— California Trail

© RMCN & CO.

a

◀ *The constant traffic of settlers to the Oregon Country marked a trail across the Great Plains and Rocky Mountains. Traders and trappers blazed other trails that settlers later followed to the Far West.*

The Mexican War 1846–1848

0   100   200 miles

✕ Battle site

© RMCN & CO.

b

◀ *The Mexican War began with a dispute over the southern boundary of Texas—the area shown in pink on the map. It ended when General Winfield Scott defeated Santa Anna and captured Mexico City. As a result of this war, the United States gained a large territory in the southwest.*

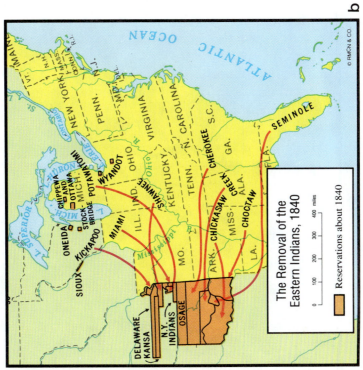

The Removal of the Eastern Indians, 1840

Reservations about 1840

0 100 200 300 400 miles

▲ The U.S. government forced Native Americans to leave their lands in the East and move to reservations in the West. The journey of 15,000 Cherokees from Georgia to Oklahoma became known as the Trail of Tears. About 4,000 Indians died along the way.

© RMCN & CO.

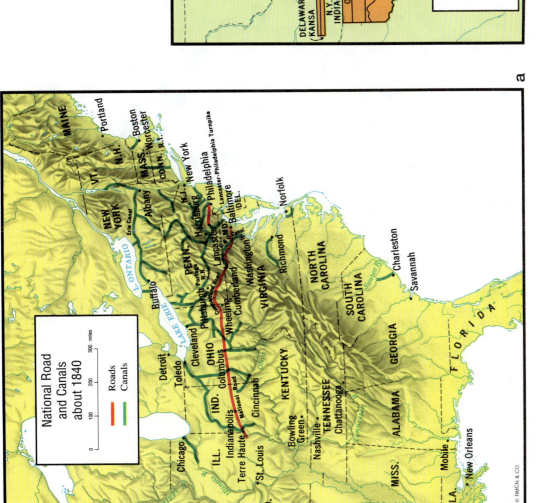

National Road and Canals about 1840

Roads
Canals

0 100 200 300 miles

▲ The Cumberland Road, also called the National Road, extended from Maryland to Illinois. The Erie Canal provided a link between the Great Lakes and the Atlantic Ocean.

© RMCN & CO.

WESTWARD EXPANSION
1800-1850

0 50 100   200   300   400

▮	U.S. Territory 1783
▮	Louisiana Purchase, 1803
▮	Texas, 1845
▮	Oregon Country
▮	Mexican Cession, 1848
IOWA 1846	States admitted 1800-1850
- - - - -	Mexican War Campaigns
———	Western Trails
✕	Battles of Mexican War
+++++	Railroads of 1850
▭▭▭	Major Canals of 1850

▶ Between 1800 and 1850, the United States added fifteen new states and extended its borders to the Pacific Coast.

Copyright by Rand McNally & Company, Made in U.S.A.

N O R T H   A M E R I C A

Quebec

Montreal

St. Lawrence

Boundary adjusted with Great Britain 1842

MAINE 1824

Lake Superior

1818

Ft. Snelling

Louisiana Purchase, 1803

Mississippi

WISCONSIN 1848

MICHIGAN 1837

Lake Michigan

Lake Huron

Milwaukee

Detroit

Lake Erie

Buffalo

Lake Ontario

VT. N.H. MASS. CONN. R.I.

NEW YORK

Boston

Chicago

IOWA 1846

Nauvoo

Mormon Trail

St. Joseph

Ft. Leavenworth

Independence

Council Grove

MISSOURI 1821

St. Louis

ILLINOIS 1818

INDIANA 1816

OHIO 1803

Cumberland Road

Cincinnati

Louisville

Ohio

PENNSYLVANIA

Pittsburgh

MD. DEL.

New York

Philadelphia

N.J.

Baltimore

Washington

KENTUCKY

Cumberland

VIRGINIA

TENNESSEE

Tennessee

NORTH CAROLINA

APPALACHIAN

SOUTH CAROLINA

Charleston

Ft. Smith

ARKANSAS 1836

Red

MISSISSIPPI 1817

ALABAMA 1819

GEORGIA

Galveston

LOUISIANA 1812

Sabine

1813

1810

West Florida seized

New Orleans

FLORIDA 1845

Annexed 1819-1821

Gulf of Mexico

Atlantic Ocean

Scott

SETTLEMENT

MILES 0 100 200 400

1820

1850

Portland

Pacific Ocean

San Francisco

Monterey

Los Angeles

Salt Lake City

Santa Fe

Chicago

St. Louis

Montreal

Philadelphia

Washington

Boston

New York

Charleston

New Orleans

Atlantic Ocean

Gulf of Mexico

▶ By 1850 settlement had spread west of the Mississippi River. Thousands of settlers also moved to the Far West.

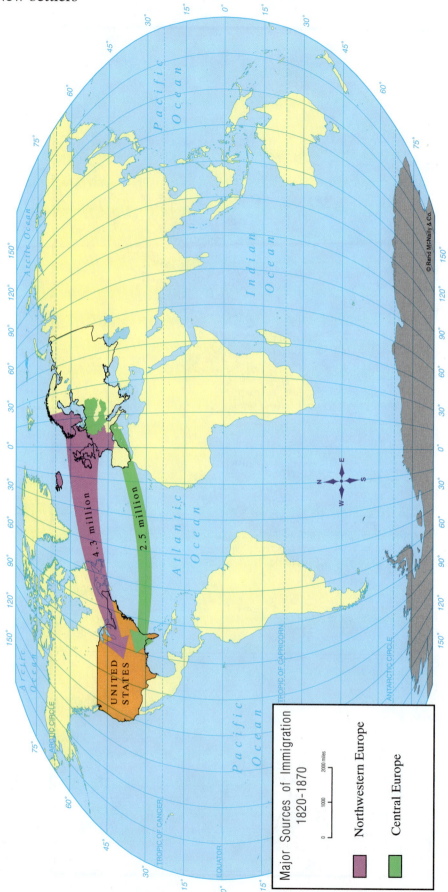

Major Sources of Immigration 1820–1870

Northwestern Europe

Central Europe

4.3 million

2.5 million

UNITED STATES

▲ *Between 1820 and 1870, about 7.5 million immigrants came to the United States. Most came from northern and western Europe. Crop failure and poverty led Irish, German, and Scandinavian immigrants to seek a better life in America.*

Section 5 (1850-1865)

A Nation Divided

Between 1850 and 1860, differences between the North and the South widened. The agricultural economy of the South was based on slave labor. Many Northerners viewed slavery as wrong. **Abolitionists**, or people who demanded an end to slavery, operated the Underground Railroad to help slaves escape. The Compromise of 1850 and the Kansas-Nebraska Act attempted to settle the issue of slavery in the West.

When Abraham Lincoln was elected president in 1860, Southerners feared he would end slavery. Eleven southern states **seceded**, or withdrew, from the Union and formed the Confederacy. An attack on Fort Sumter in April 1861 marked the beginning of the Civil War. The war ended when Confederate general Robert E. Lee surrendered at Appomattox in April 1865.

The bitter war between the North and the South left lasting problems. Much of the South was destroyed. More Americans lost their lives in the Civil War than in any other war in which the United States has fought.

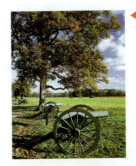

The Battle of Gettysburg took place at this site in Pennsylvania in July 1863.

This memorial to Confederate leaders is carved on Stone Mountain near Atlanta, Georgia.

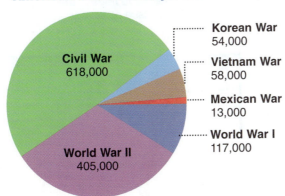

American Deaths in Major Wars

- Civil War 618,000
- World War II 405,000
- Korean War 54,000
- Vietnam War 58,000
- Mexican War 13,000
- World War I 117,000

Did You Know?

When Virginia seceded from the Union in 1861, 50 of its western counties separated from the state. These counties were admitted to the Union in 1863 as the state of West Virginia.

People

1850 — Harriet Tubman leads slaves from Maryland to freedom in the North.

1863 — Abraham Lincoln delivers Gettysburg Address on battlefield in Pennsylvania.

1865 — Robert E. Lee surrenders at Appomattox Court House, Virginia.

Events

1860 — South Carolina becomes first southern state to secede.

1861 — Civil War begins at Fort Sumter, South Carolina.

1865 — Thirteenth Amendment ends slavery in the United States.

Literature

1850 — *The Scarlet Letter*, by Nathaniel Hawthorne, is set in Puritan New England.

1852 — *Uncle Tom's Cabin*, by Harriet Beecher Stowe, highlights the cruelty of slavery in the South.

1865 — "Drum Taps," by Walt Whitman, describes scenes from Civil War battlefields.

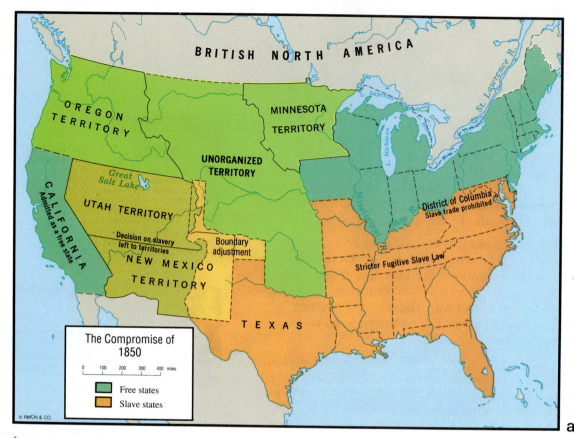

The Compromise of 1850

0 100 200 300 400 miles

Free states

Slave states

▲ The Compromise of 1850 admitted California as a free state and ended slave trade in the District of Columbia. Utah and New Mexico Territories could decide the issue of slavery.

Kansas–Nebraska Act, 1854

0 100 200 300 miles

▲ The Kansas-Nebraska Act allowed settlers in those territories to decide whether to allow slavery.

b

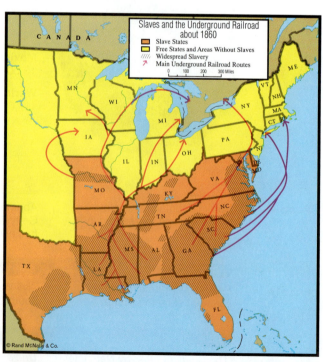

Slaves and the Underground Railroad about 1860

Slave States

Free States and Areas Without Slaves

Widespread Slavery

Main Underground Railroad Routes

0 100 200 300 Miles

▲ The Underground Railroad was a system of escape routes slaves followed to freedom.

c

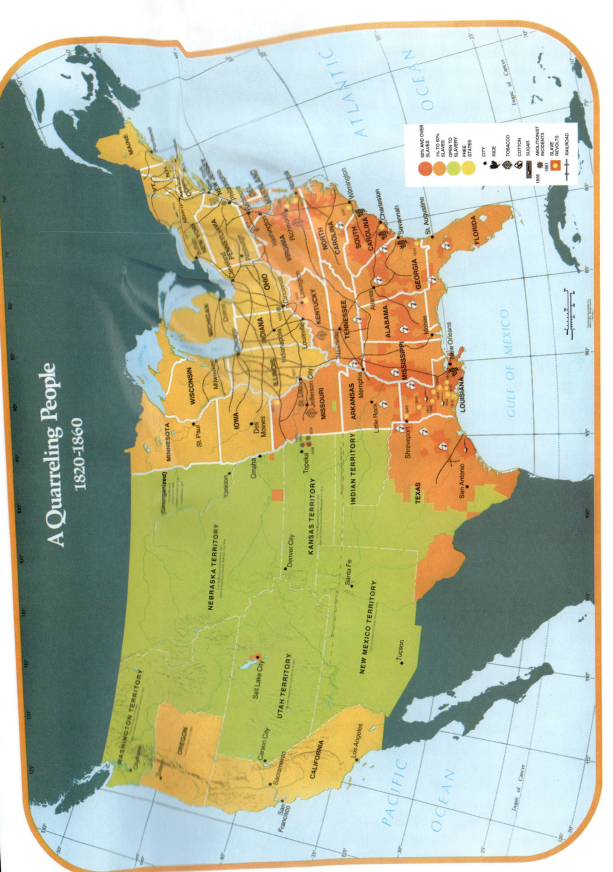

A Quarreling People
1820-1860

Legend:

- 50% AND OVER SLAVES
- 1% TO 50% SLAVES
- OPEN TO SLAVERY
- FREE STATES
- CITY
- RICE
- TOBACCO
- COTTON
- SUGAR
- ABOLITIONIST INCIDENTS 1835
- SLAVE REVOLTS 1851
- RAILROAD

States and Territories: MAINE, VT., N.H., MASS., R.I., CONN., NEW YORK, PENNSYLVANIA, NEW JERSEY, DEL., MARYLAND, OHIO, INDIANA, ILLINOIS, MICHIGAN, WISCONSIN, MINNESOTA, IOWA, MISSOURI, KENTUCKY, VIRGINIA, NORTH CAROLINA, SOUTH CAROLINA, GEORGIA, FLORIDA, ALABAMA, MISSISSIPPI, TENNESSEE, ARKANSAS, LOUISIANA, TEXAS, NEBRASKA TERRITORY, KANSAS TERRITORY, INDIAN TERRITORY, NEW MEXICO TERRITORY, UTAH TERRITORY, WASHINGTON TERRITORY, OREGON, CALIFORNIA, (Unorganized)

Cities: New York, Philadelphia, Pittsburgh, Baltimore, Washington, Richmond, Wilmington, Charleston, Savannah, St. Augustine, Cincinnati, Indianapolis, Louisville, Nashville, Memphis, Atlanta, Mobile, New Orleans, Shreveport, Little Rock, Jefferson City, St. Louis, Des Moines, St. Paul, Milwaukee, Detroit, Cleveland, Columbus, Omaha, Topeka, Denver City, Santa Fe, Tucson, San Antonio, Los Angeles, Salt Lake City, Carson City, Sacramento, San Francisco, Olympia

Oceans: ATLANTIC OCEAN, PACIFIC OCEAN, GULF OF MEXICO

Tropic of Cancer

▲ *Economic differences created different ways of life in the North and the South. Plantation crops, such as tobacco, cotton, and sugar cane, supported an agricultural economy based on slavery in the South. Advances in mass production and transportation supported an economy based on industry and trade in the North. Northern abolitionists viewed slavery as wrong and began a movement to end it.*

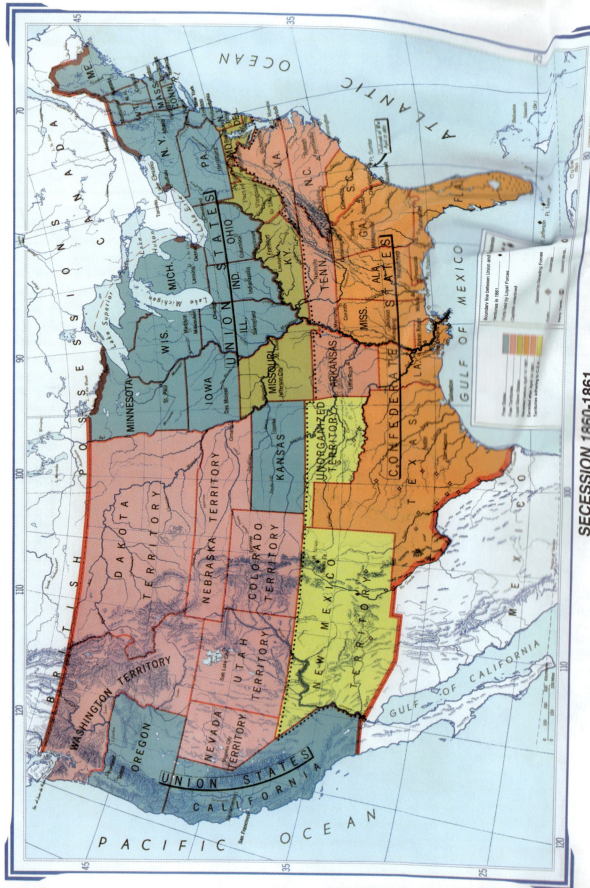

SECESSION 1860-1861

▲ The Confederate States of America consisted of eleven slave states that seceded from the Union in 1860 and 1861. The 23 remaining states and territories, including four slave states, fought for the Union during the Civil War.

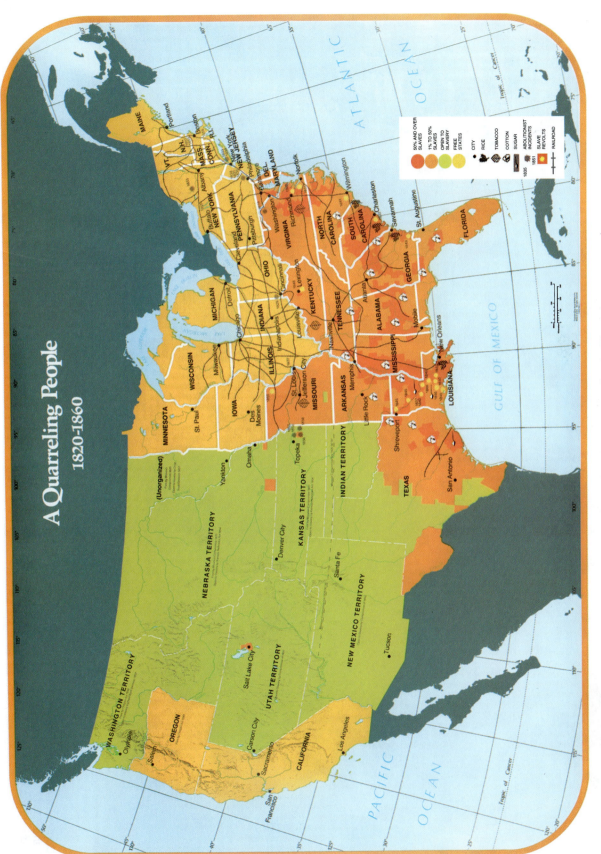

A Quarreling People
1820–1860

LEGEND

- 50% AND OVER SLAVES
- 1% TO 50% SLAVES
- OPEN TO SLAVERY
- FREE STATES
- CITY
- RICE
- TOBACCO
- COTTON
- SUGAR
- ABOLITIONIST INCIDENTS 1835
- SLAVE REVOLTS 1851
- RAILROAD

▲ *Economic differences created different ways of life in the North and the South. Plantation crops, such as tobacco, cotton, and sugar cane, supported an agricultural economy based on slavery in the South. Advances in mass production and transportation supported an economy based on industry and trade in the North. Northern abolitionists viewed slavery as wrong and began a movement to end it.*

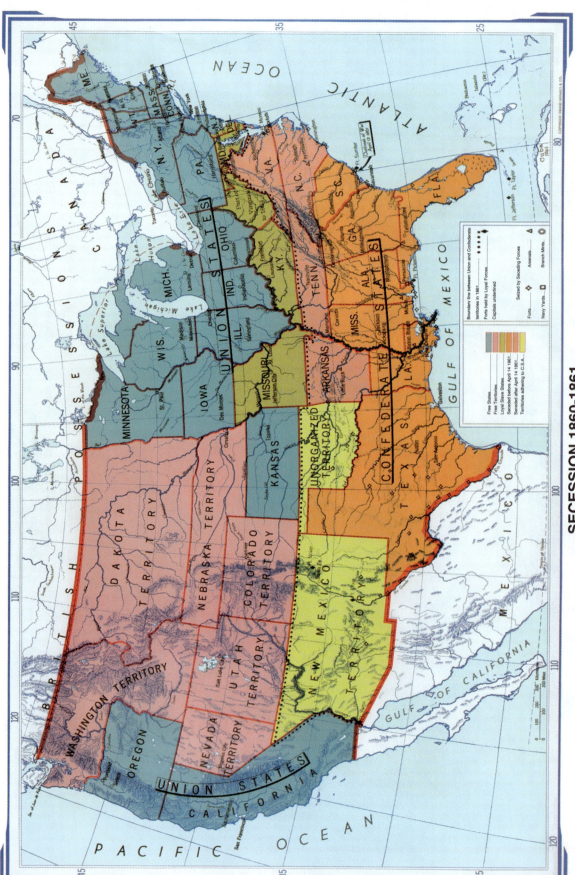

SECESSION 1860-1861

The Confederate States of America consisted of eleven slave states that seceded from the Union in 1860 and 1861. The 23 remaining states and territories, including four slave states, fought for the Union during the Civil War.

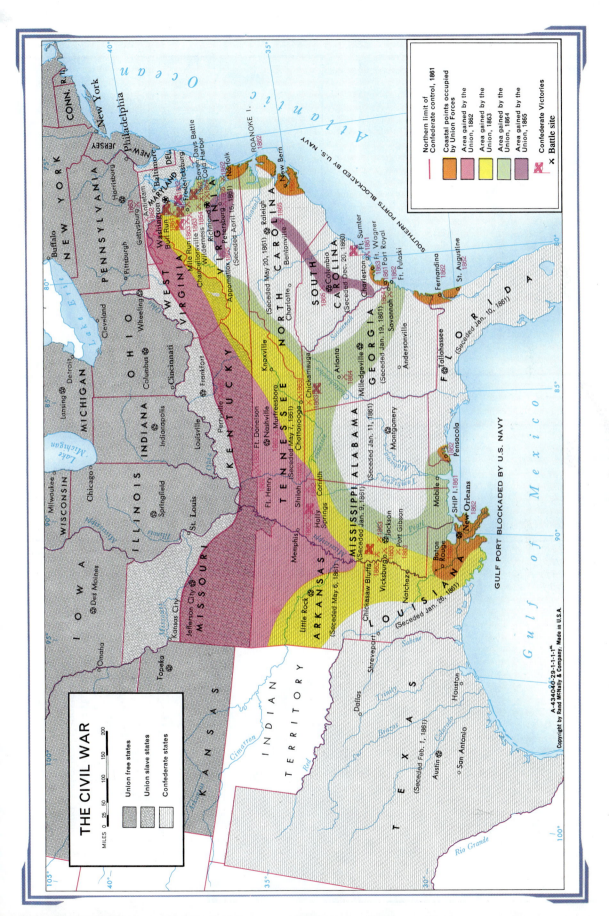

THE CIVIL WAR

MILES 0 25 50 100 150 200

- Union free states
- Union slave states
- Confederate states

Northern limit of Confederate control, 1861
Coastal points occupied by Union Forces
Area gained by the Union, 1862
Area gained by the Union, 1863
Area gained by the Union, 1864
Area gained by the Union, 1865
Confederate Victories
× Battle site

▲ *Most of the fighting in the East took place in Virginia. Much of the fighting in the West took place in Tennessee and along the Mississippi River. The map legend indicates how Union strategy succeeded by dividing the Confederacy and blockading its ports.*

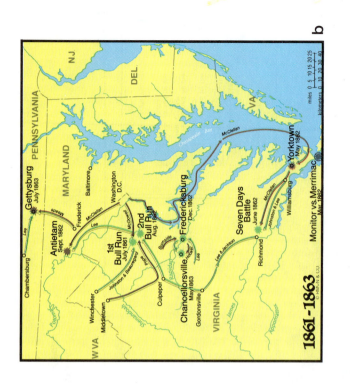

1861-1863

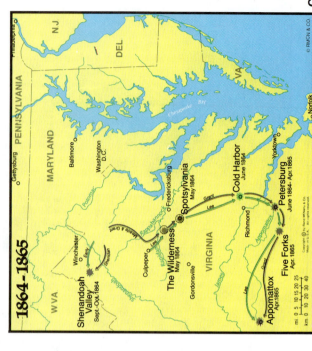

1864-1865

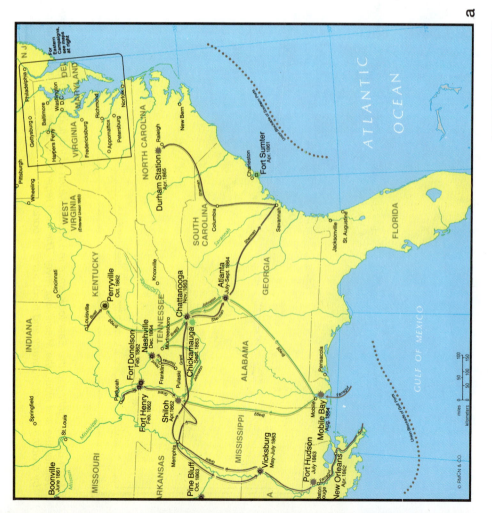

The Civil War 1861–1865

- Union victory
- Confederate victory
- Battle indecisive
- Union forces
- Confederate forces

Union strategy involved blockading southern ports, splitting the Confederacy by gaining control of the Mississippi River Valley, and capturing Richmond. Confederate strategy involved defending the South from attack, breaking the Union blockade, and splitting the Union by gaining control of Washington, D.C., Maryland, and central Pennsylvania.

Section 6   *(1860-1920)*

Emerging as a Modern Nation

The years between 1860 and 1920 included the end of one era in American history and the beginning of another. The Great Plains opened to settlers as the U.S. Army defeated the Plains Indians and forced them onto reservations. Texas cattle ranchers drove their herds to railroads, which provided transportation to eastern markets. **Homesteaders**, or settlers who received free land from the government in exchange for farming it, moved to western territories. By 1890, the long process of settling the United States from coast to coast was complete. The American frontier had come to an end.

In the late 1800s, the United States began to emerge as a modern nation. Millions of immigrants came from Europe to farm the land or work in factories. The United States became an industrial nation and acquired territories overseas. It purchased Alaska and established naval bases on islands in the Pacific. It fought a war with Spain by which it acquired additional territories. The United States entered World War I in 1917 and assumed its role as a world power.

◀ This statue of Buffalo Bill Cody in Wyoming represents the Old West.

The Statue of Liberty ▶ in New York Harbor has welcomed immigrants since 1886. It was a gift to the United States from France.

Immigration to the United States, 1860-1919

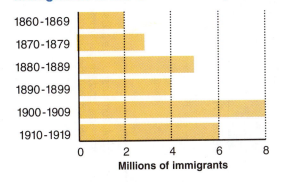

Period	Millions of immigrants
1860-1869	2
1870-1879	2.7
1880-1889	5
1890-1899	4
1900-1909	8
1910-1919	6

Millions of immigrants (0 – 2 – 4 – 6 – 8)

Did You Know ?

In 1850 about 20 million bison, or buffaloes, roamed the Great Plains. The westward movement almost wiped out these animals. By 1890, only about 500 bison could be found in the West.

People

1877 Chief Joseph leads Nez Percés on a retreat through Idaho and Montana.

1889 Jane Addams opens Hull House to help immigrants in Chicago.

1898 Theodore Roosevelt leads Rough Riders in Cuba during Spanish-American War.

Events

1867 United States purchases Alaska from Russia.

1892 Ellis Island, in New York Harbor, becomes an immigration station.

1898 Hawaii becomes a U.S. territory.

Literature

1876 *The Adventures of Tom Sawyer*, by Mark Twain, is set in Hannibal, Missouri.

1881 *A Century of Dishonor*, by Helen Hunt Jackson, describes mistreatment of Native Americans in the U.S.

1912 *Riders of the Purple Sage*, by Zane Grey, describes life in the West.

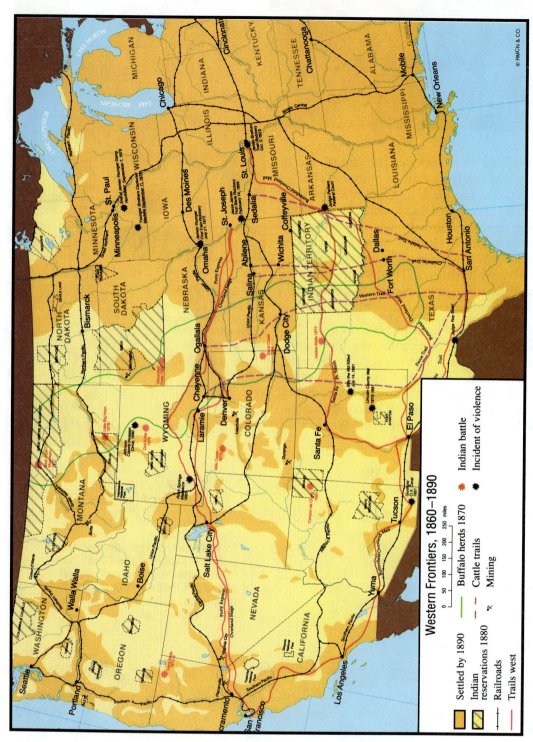

Western Frontiers, 1860–1890

Settled by 1890

Indian reservations 1880

Railroads

Trails west

Buffalo herds 1870

Cattle trails

Mining

Indian battle

Incident of violence

0 50 100 150 200 250 miles

After 1860, the population west of the Mississippi River grew rapidly. Native Americans lost the battle to keep their lands, and the government moved them to reservations. Ranchers and farmers spread settlements throughout the Great Plains and the Far West. Although large areas of the West remained thinly populated, in 1890 the Census Bureau declared the frontier had come to an end.

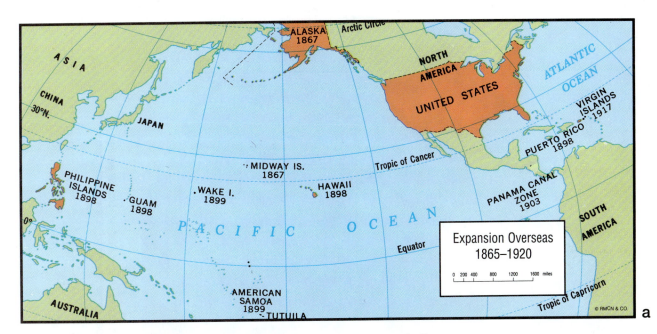

▲ The United States acquired islands in the Pacific Ocean that served as fueling stations for ships traveling to and from China and Japan. The Hawaiian Islands also provided raw materials for import or trade.

▲ The sinking of the American battleship *Maine* in Havana harbor brought the United States into war with Spain. The war was fought in both Cuba and the Philippines. As a result of the Spanish-American War, Spain granted freedom to Cuba and ceded Guam, Puerto Rico, and the Philippines to the United States.

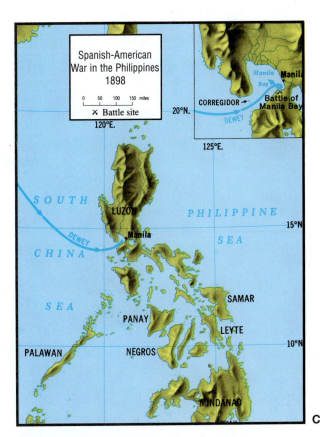

▲ In the Battle of Manila Bay, American ships commanded by Commodore George Dewey destroyed the Spanish fleet in the Philippines.

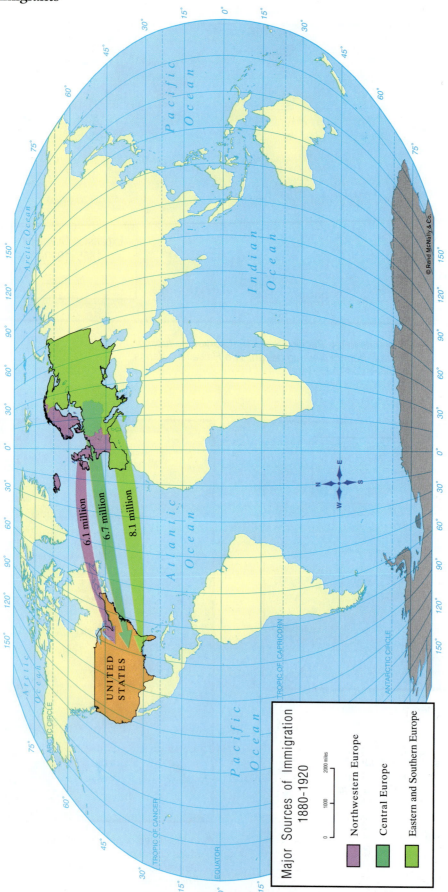

Major Sources of Immigration 1880–1920

Northwestern Europe

Central Europe

Eastern and Southern Europe

0   1000   2000 miles

UNITED STATES

6.1 million

6.7 million

8.1 million

▲ Between 1880 and 1920, more than 20 million immigrants came to the United States. Unlike earlier newcomers, who came mostly from northern and western Europe, these so-called "new immigrants" came mostly from central, eastern, and southern Europe.

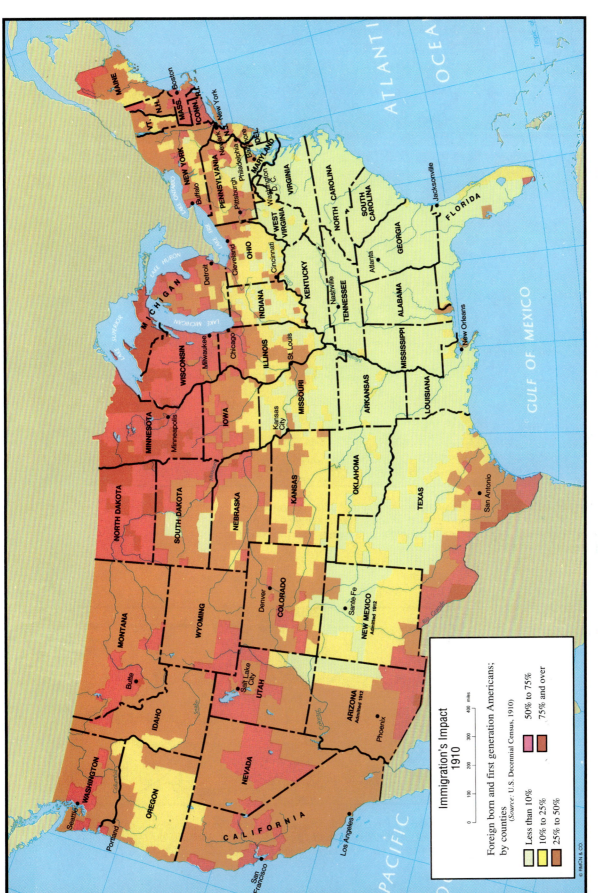

Immigration's Impact 1910

Foreign born and first generation Americans; by counties

(*Source:* U.S. Decennial Census, 1910)

Less than 10%	50% to 75%
10% to 25%	75% and over
25% to 50%	

0 100 200 300 400 miles

© RMCN & CO.

▲ Many immigrants settled in large cities in the East. Mining attracted newcomers to Montana, Colorado, and Nevada. Railroad companies encouraged European workers to settle in the West. Poor economic conditions in Mexico led thousands of immigrants to settle in the United States.

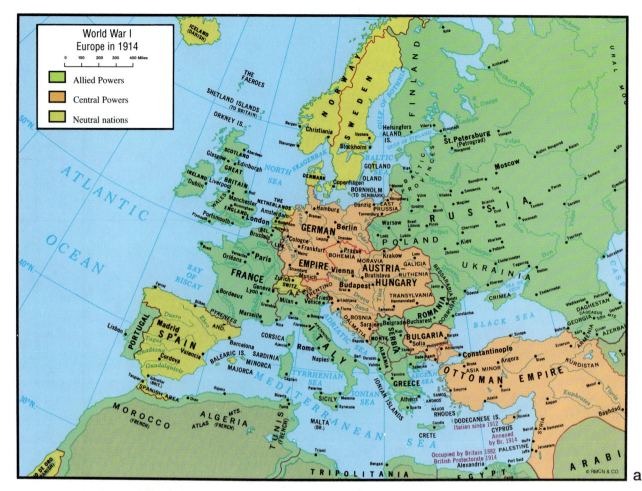

▲ In 1914, long-standing problems in Europe erupted in war between the Allied Powers and the Central Powers. The conflict, which became known as World War I, lasted four years. It involved more countries and caused more destruction than had any previous war.

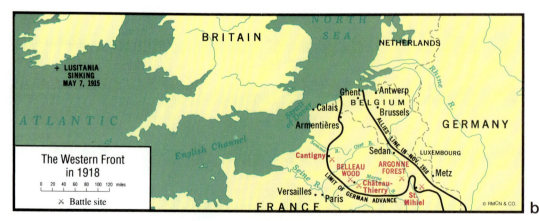

▲ The loss of American lives aboard the Lusitania helped draw the United States into the war in Europe. American troops helped the Allies defeat the Germans on the Western Front, which stretched through Belgium and France.

Section 7 *(1920-1990)*

Challenges & Changes in the 20th Century

During the decades between 1920 and 1990, the United States faced many challenges and experienced many changes. The economic prosperity of the 1920s ended with the stock market crash in 1929. Poverty and unemployment were widespread during the Great Depression of the 1930s. During World War II (1941-1945), United States troops fought in Europe and in the Pacific. After this war, the United States and the Soviet Union emerged as the world's leading powers.

The struggle between the Communist world, led by the Soviet Union, and the free world, led by the United States, was called the **Cold War**. Between 1950 and 1990, the United States intervened in Korea, in Southeast Asia, and in Central America and the Caribbean to stop the spread of communism.

Changes took place within the United States as Americans moved from one area of the country to another, and suburbs grew around major cities. The **gross domestic product** (GDP), or value of all goods and services produced within the country, rose sharply after 1940. Economic growth continued into the 1990s.

The United States Marine Corps Memorial in Arlington, Virginia, honors the flag raising on Iwo Jima during World War II.

In 1940 Houston, Texas, ranked 21st in population among U.S. cities. By 1990, it was among the nation's largest metropolitan areas.

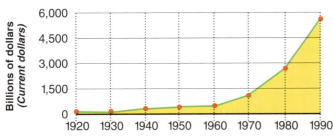

Gross Domestic Product, 1920-1990

Did You Know?

Between 1941 and 1945, one in every five Americans moved from one part of the United States to another.

People

1927 Charles Lindbergh makes first nonstop flight from New York to Paris.

1963 Dr. Martin Luther King, Jr., leads civil rights march on Washington, D.C.

1981 Arizona judge Sandra Day O'Connor becomes first woman to serve on the Supreme Court.

Events

1959 Alaska and Hawaii become states.

1961 First American astronaut is launched into space from Cape Canaveral, Florida.

1973 Native Americans seize Wounded Knee, South Dakota, to demand return of Indian lands.

Literature

1939 *The Grapes of Wrath*, by John Steinbeck, tells of an Oklahoma family during the Great Depression.

1961 *To Kill a Mockingbird*, by Harper Lee, explores racial prejudice in Alabama.

1971 *Barrio Boy*, by Ernesto Galarza, describes Hispanic life in Sacramento, California.

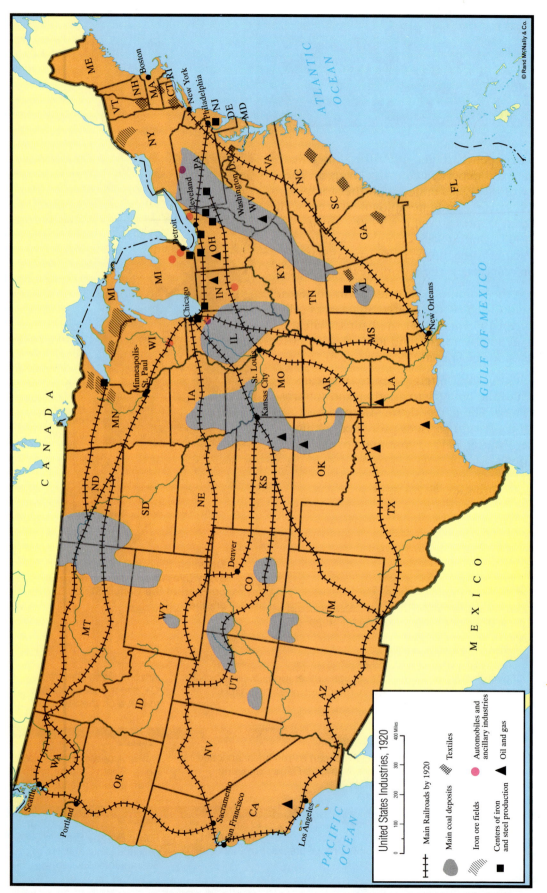

© Rand McNally & Co.

ATLANTIC OCEAN

GULF OF MEXICO

PACIFIC OCEAN

CANADA

MEXICO

ME
NH
VT
MA
CT RI
NY
New York
Boston
Philadelphia
NJ
DE
MD
PA
Cleveland
Washington, D.C.
VA
WV
NC
SC
GA
FL
Detroit
OH
MI
IN
KY
TN
AL
New Orleans
MS
LA
Chicago
IL
WI
Minneapolis-St. Paul
IA
MO
AR
OK
St. Louis
Kansas City
ND
SD
NE
KS
TX
MN
Denver
CO
WY
NM
AZ
UT
MT
ID
NV
OR
CA
Sacramento
San Francisco
Los Angeles
Seattle
Portland

▶ By 1920 the United States was a leading industrial nation. Advances in technology enabled workers to produce more goods faster. The demand for petroleum and steel increased to meet the growing needs of new industries such as the automobile industry. Spectacular economic growth provided a high standard of living for many Americans.

United States Industries, 1920

┼┼┼┼	Main Railroads by 1920
(gray)	Main coal deposits
(hatched)	Iron ore fields
■	Centers of iron and steel production
▨	Textiles
●	Automobiles and ancillary industries
▲	Oil and gas

0 100 200 300 400 Miles

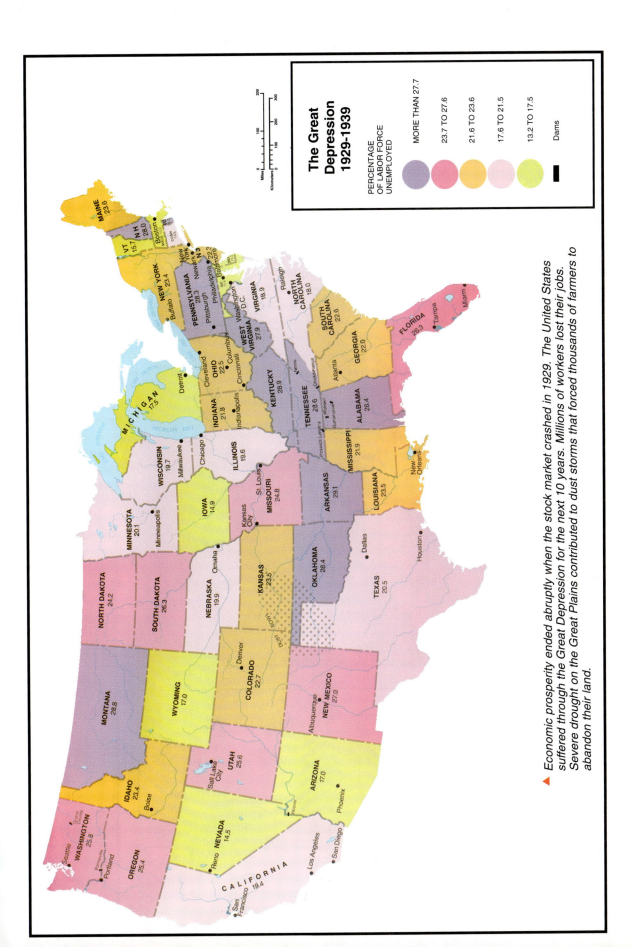

The Great Depression 1929-1939

PERCENTAGE
OF LABOR FORCE
UNEMPLOYED

- MORE THAN 27.7
- 23.7 TO 27.6
- 21.6 TO 23.6
- 17.6 TO 21.5
- 13.2 TO 17.5
- Dams

▲ *Economic prosperity ended abruptly when the stock market crashed in 1929. The United States suffered through the Great Depression for the next 10 years. Millions of workers lost their jobs. Severe drought on the Great Plains contributed to dust storms that forced thousands of farmers to abandon their land.*

MAINE 23.6
N.H. 28.0
VT 15.7
Boston
New York
N.J.
Newark
NEW YORK 23.4
Buffalo
PENNSYLVANIA 28.3
Pittsburgh
Philadelphia 22.3
Baltimore
Washington D.C.
WEST VIRGINIA 27.9
VIRGINIA 18.9
NORTH CAROLINA 18.0
Raleigh
SOUTH CAROLINA 22.6
GEORGIA 22.0
Atlanta
FLORIDA 26.3
Tampa
Miami
OHIO 22.5
Columbus
Cincinnati
Cleveland
INDIANA 21.8
Indianapolis
KENTUCKY 28.9
TENNESSEE 28.6
ALABAMA 28.4
MISSISSIPPI 21.9
Detroit
MICHIGAN 17.5
WISCONSIN 19.7
Milwaukee
Chicago
ILLINOIS 19.6
IOWA 14.9
St. Louis
MISSOURI 24.8
Kansas City
ARKANSAS 29.1
LOUISIANA 23.5
New Orleans
MINNESOTA 20.1
Minneapolis
Omaha
NEBRASKA 19.9
KANSAS 23.5
OKLAHOMA 28.4
Dallas
Houston
TEXAS 20.5
NORTH DAKOTA 24.2
SOUTH DAKOTA 26.3
Denver
COLORADO 22.7
NEW MEXICO 27.0
Albuquerque
MONTANA 28.8
WYOMING 17.0
UTAH 25.6
Salt Lake City
IDAHO 23.4
Boise
ARIZONA 17.0
Phoenix
NEVADA 14.5
Reno
Seattle
WASHINGTON 25.8
Portland
OREGON 25.4
Los Angeles
San Diego
CALIFORNIA 19.4
San Francisco

Miles
Kilometers
100 200
100 200 300

SOVIET UNION
(non-belligerent in Pacific War)

ALASKA

Dutch Harbor

ATTU
KISKA   ALEUTIAN IS.

9 days

12 days

CHINA

Chungking   Shanghai

Tokyo
JAPAN

PACIFIC

San
Franci

Karachi

INDIA
Calcutta   BURMA   Kunming

Hong Kong

PHILIPPINE IS.
To Japan
April 1942

Prince of
Wales sunk
Dec. 1941

Singapore

To Japan
Feb. 1942

DUTCH EAST INDIES

INDIAN

OCEAN

MIDWAY IS.
June 1942

WAKE I.

GUAM

MARSHALL IS.

CAROLINE IS.

Pearl Harbor
Dec. 1941   HAWAIIAN IS.

8 days

67 hours

OCEA

Rabaul
SOLOMON IS.

GUADALCANAL
Aug. 1942

Coral Sea
May
1942

NEW CALEDONIA

26 days

AUSTRALIA
Brisbane

Sydney

28 days

NEW ZEALAND

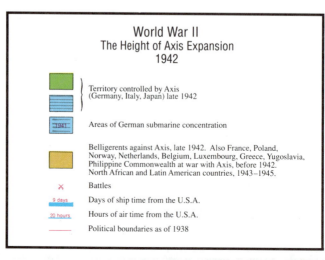

**World War II
The Height of Axis Expansion
1942**

Territory controlled by Axis
(Germany, Italy, Japan) late 1942

1941   Areas of German submarine concentration

Belligerents against Axis, late 1942. Also France, Poland,
Norway, Netherlands, Belgium, Luxembourg, Greece, Yugoslavia,
Philippine Commonwealth at war with Axis, before 1942.
North African and Latin American countries, 1943–1945.

✕   Battles

9 days   Days of ship time from the U.S.A.

20 hours   Hours of air time from the U.S.A.

Political boundaries as of 1938

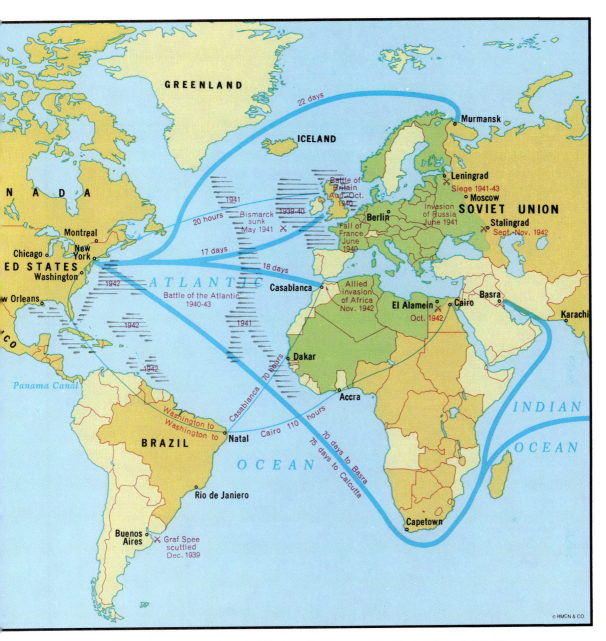

GREENLAND

ICELAND

22 days

Murmansk

Leningrad
Siege 1941-43
Moscow

SOVIET UNION

Battle of
Britain
Aug.-Oct.
1940

Berlin

Invasion
of Russia
June 1941

Stalingrad
Sept.-Nov. 1942

CANADA

1941

Bismarck
sunk
May 1941

1939-40

20 hours

Montreal

17 days

Fall of
France
1940

Chicago
New
York

18 days

Washington

ATLANTIC

ED STATES

1942

Battle of the Atlantic
1940-43

Casablanca

Allied
invasion
of Africa
Nov. 1942

El Alamein
Oct. 1942

Cairo

Basra

Karachi

w Orleans

MEXICO

1942

1941

Dakar

INDIAN

1942

Casablanca to 70 hours

Accra

Panama Canal

Washington to
Washington to

Natal

Cairo 110 hours

70 days to Basra

OCEAN

BRAZIL

75 days to Calcutta

OCEAN

Rio de Janiero

Buenos
Aires

Graf Spee
scuttled
Dec. 1939

Capetown

© RMCN & CO.

▲ World War II began in 1939 when Germany, under Nazi dictator Adolf Hitler, invaded Poland. The Axis powers (Germany, Italy, Japan, and their partners) fought against the Allied powers (shown in gold on the map). Few nations remained neutral. By 1942 the Axis controlled most of Europe, northern Africa, and parts of Asia and the Pacific. German submarines attacked Allied cargo ships in the Atlantic.

The Japanese attack on Pearl Harbor, Hawaii, in December 1941 brought the United States into the war. American troops and supplies were sent to Europe and to the Pacific. The map indicates transportation time by air and by water from the United States to selected sites. During 1942, Allied forces halted Axis expansion in northern Africa, the Soviet Union, and the Pacific.

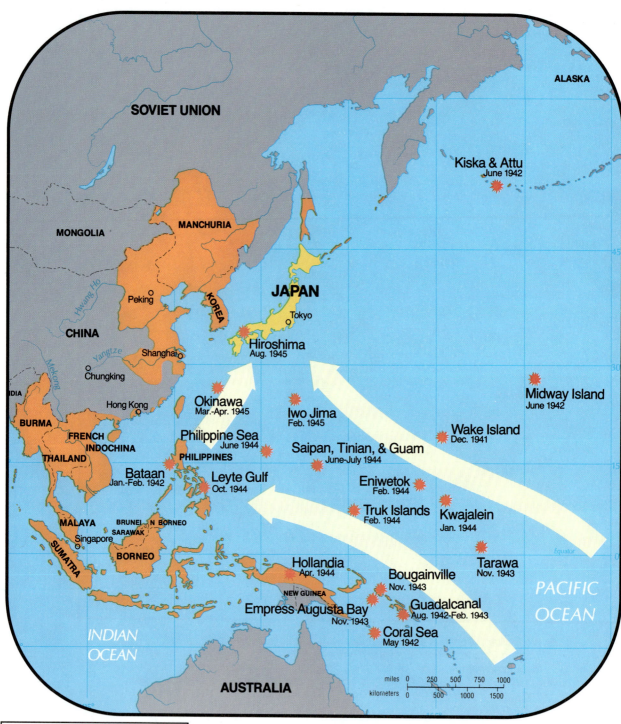

SOVIET UNION

ALASKA

MONGOLIA

MANCHURIA

Peking

CHINA

Hwang Ho

Yangtze

Chungking

Shanghai

Mekong

KOREA

JAPAN

Tokyo

Hiroshima
Aug. 1945

Kiska & Attu
June 1942

Midway Island
June 1942

IDIA

BURMA

FRENCH
INDOCHINA

THAILAND

Hong Kong

Okinawa
Mar.-Apr. 1945

Iwo Jima
Feb. 1945

Wake Island
Dec. 1941

Philippine Sea
June 1944

Saipan, Tinian, & Guam
June-July 1944

Bataan
Jan.-Feb. 1942

PHILIPPINES

Leyte Gulf
Oct. 1944

Eniwetok
Feb. 1944

Truk Islands
Feb. 1944

Kwajalein
Jan. 1944

MALAYA

BRUNEI

N BORNEO

SARAWAK

Singapore

BORNEO

SUMATRA

Hollandia
Apr. 1944

Tarawa
Nov. 1943

Bougainville
Nov. 1943

NEW GUINEA

Empress Augusta Bay
Nov. 1943

Guadalcanal
Aug. 1942-Feb. 1943

Equator

PACIFIC
OCEAN

INDIAN
OCEAN

Coral Sea
May 1942

AUSTRALIA

miles	0	250	500	750	1000
kilometers	0	500	1000	1500	

World War II
1941–1945
Pacific Theater

Allied powers

Axis powers — Battles

Axis controlled
areas — Allied advances

▲ In 1943 and 1944, the Allies captured
Japanese-held islands in the Pacific. In
August 1945, the United States dropped
an atomic bomb on Hiroshima, Japan.
World War II ended when the Japanese
surrendered in September 1945.

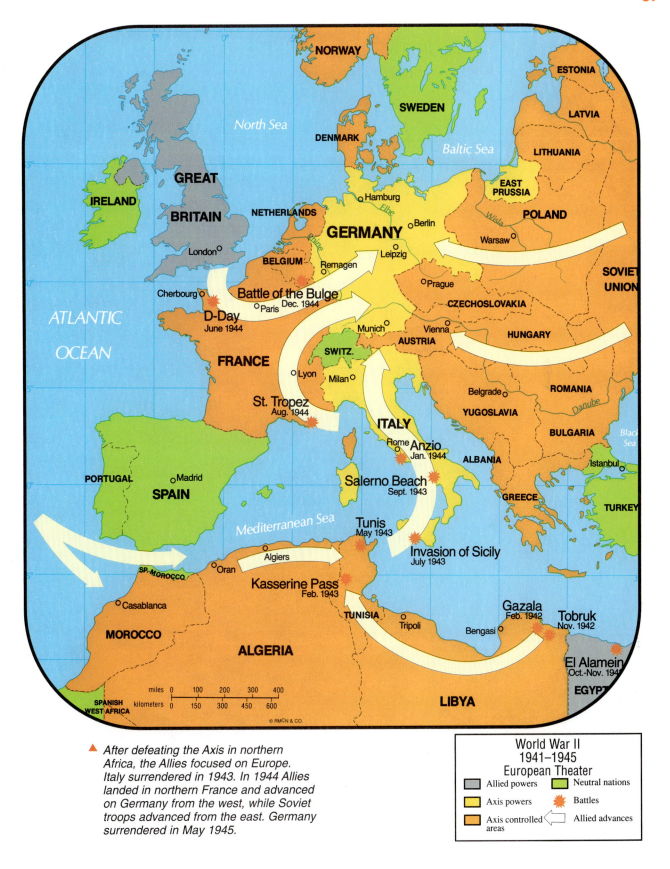

NORWAY

SWEDEN

ESTONIA

LATVIA

DENMARK

LITHUANIA

North Sea

Baltic Sea

GREAT

IRELAND

BRITAIN

EAST
PRUSSIA

POLAND

NETHERLANDS

Hamburg

GERMANY

Berlin

Warsaw

London

BELGIUM

Leipzig

SOVIET
UNION

Remagen

Cherbourg

Battle of the Bulge
Dec. 1944

Paris

Prague

CZECHOSLOVAKIA

D-Day
June 1944

ATLANTIC

OCEAN

FRANCE

Munich

Vienna

AUSTRIA

HUNGARY

SWITZ.

Lyon

Milan

St. Tropez
Aug. 1944

ITALY

Belgrade

ROMANIA

YUGOSLAVIA

Danube

Rome

Anzio
Jan. 1944

BULGARIA

*Black
Sea*

PORTUGAL

Madrid

Salerno Beach
Sept. 1943

ALBANIA

Istanbul

SPAIN

GREECE

TURKEY

Mediterranean Sea

Tunis
May 1943

SP. MOROCCO

Oran

Algiers

Invasion of Sicily
July 1943

Casablanca

Kasserine Pass
Feb. 1943

TUNISIA

Tripoli

Gazala
Feb. 1942

Bengasi

Tobruk
Nov. 1942

MOROCCO

ALGERIA

El Alamein
Oct.-Nov. 194

EGYPT

miles 0   100   200   300   400

SPANISH
WEST AFRICA

kilometers 0   150   300   450   600

LIBYA

© RMCN & CO.

▲ *After defeating the Axis in northern
Africa, the Allies focused on Europe.
Italy surrendered in 1943. In 1944 Allies
landed in northern France and advanced
on Germany from the west, while Soviet
troops advanced from the east. Germany
surrendered in May 1945.*

World War II
1941–1945
European Theater

Allied powers	Neutral nations
Axis powers	Battles
Axis controlled areas	Allied advances

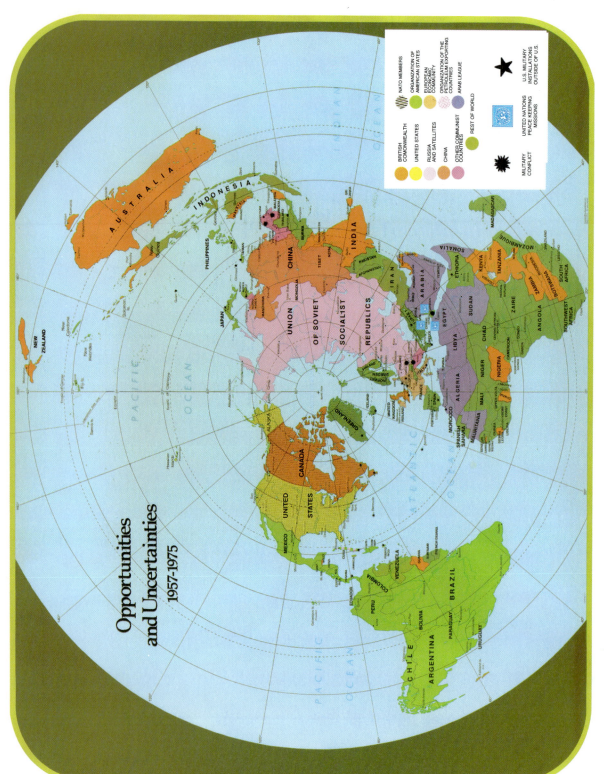

Opportunities and Uncertainties
1957-1975

▲ In 1949 the United States and other free nations formed a military alliance called the North Atlantic Treaty Organization (NATO) to prevent the spread of communism. The Soviet Union and other communist countries formed a competing alliance called the Warsaw Pact. This view indicates why Canada and the United States feared a possible Soviet attack from the north.

b

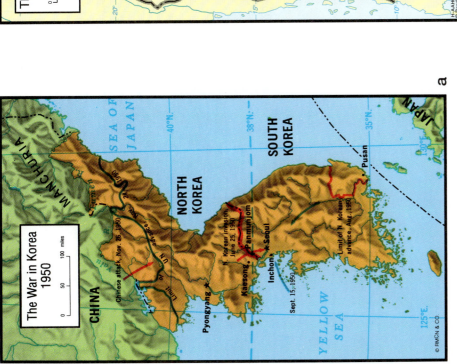

The United States entered the longest war
in its history to prevent communist-ruled
North Vietnam from taking over non-
communist South Vietnam. The Ho Chi
Minh Trail was a system of roads the
North Vietnamese used as a supply route
for the Viet Cong, or communist rebels
in South Vietnam.

a

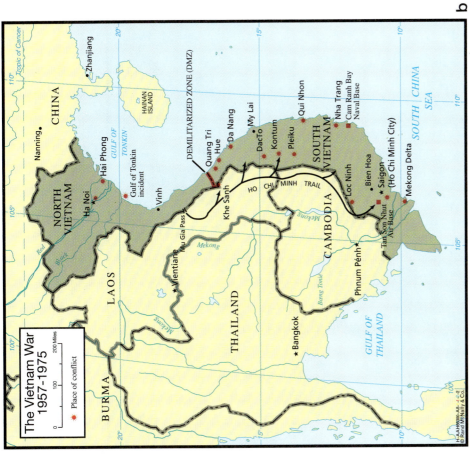

United Nations members, including the
United States, sent troops to defend
South Korea from an invasion by
communist-ruled North Korea. In 1950,
UN forces halted the North Korean
advance at Pusan and pushed to the Yalu
River in the north. The war ended in
1953 when the UN and North Korea
signed an armistice agreement.

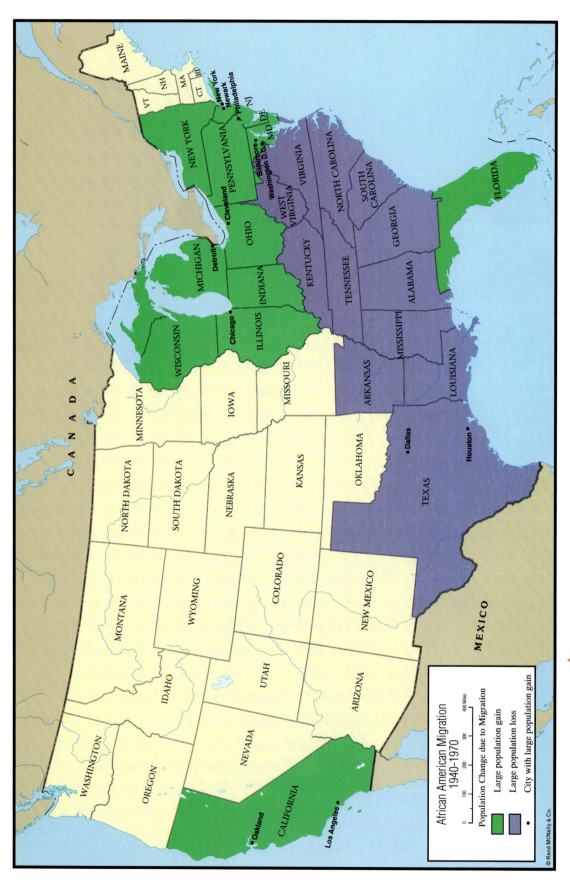

African American Migration 1940-1970

Population Change due to Migration

■ Large population gain

■ Large population loss

■ City with large population gain

0   100   200   300   400 Miles

© Rand McNally & Co.

▲ *Between 1940 and 1970, millions of African Americans moved out of the South. More than two-thirds of the total African American population relocated to cities. More than half the urban black population was concentrated in the twelve cities shown on the map.*

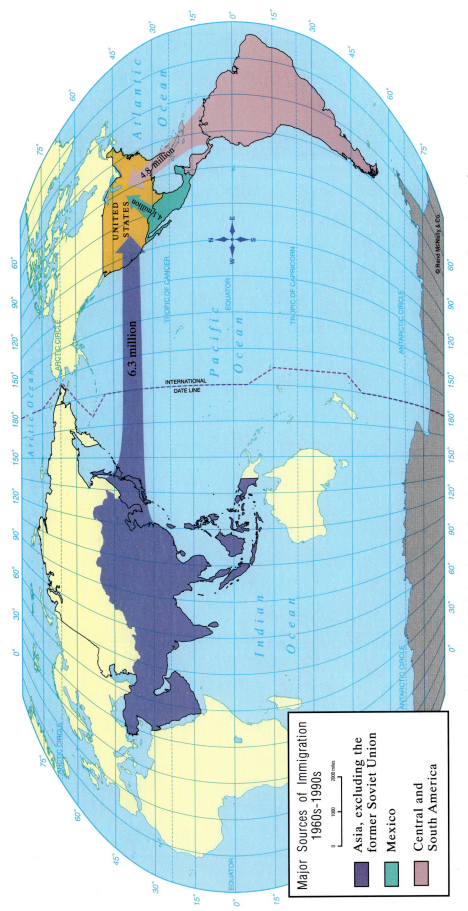

▲ Changes in U.S. immigration laws in the 1960s changed immigration patterns. Percentages of immigrants from Europe decreased. In the 1990s, most immigrants to the United States came from Mexico, the Philippines, Haiti, China, India, Vietnam, Jamaica, Cuba, and South Korea.

Major Sources of Immigration 1960s–1990s

Asia, excluding the former Soviet Union

Mexico

Central and South America

UNITED STATES

4.8 million

4.1 million

6.3 million

Atlantic Ocean

Pacific Ocean

Indian Ocean

Arctic Ocean

INTERNATIONAL DATE LINE

TROPIC OF CANCER

EQUATOR

TROPIC OF CAPRICORN

ANTARCTIC CIRCLE

ARCTIC CIRCLE

© Rand McNally & Co.

0   1000   2000 miles

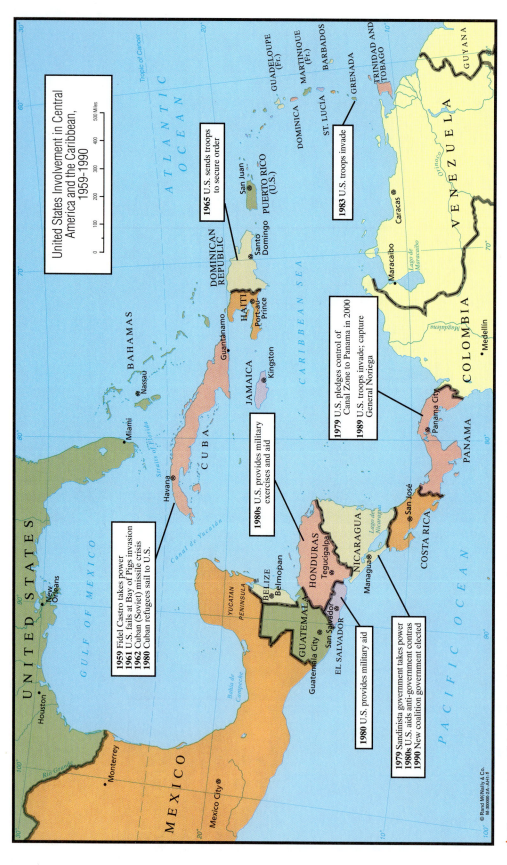

United States Involvement in Central America and the Caribbean, 1959-1990

1965 U.S. sends troops to secure order

1983 U.S. troops invade

1979 U.S. pledges control of Canal Zone to Panama in 2000
1989 U.S. troops invade; capture General Noriega

1980s U.S. provides military exercises and aid

1959 Fidel Castro takes power
1961 U.S. fails at Bay of Pigs invasion
1962 Cuban (Soviet) missile crisis
1980 Cuban refugees sail to U.S.

1980 U.S. provides military aid

1979 Sandinista government takes power
1980s U.S. aids anti-government contras
1990 New coalition government elected

© Rand McNally & Co.
M-300000-2A-AH-1

▲ *Communist activity in Central America and the Caribbean threatened U.S. security. In 1962 the Cuban missile crisis led the United States to the brink of nuclear war with the Soviet Union. The United States continued to intervene in the region to support democracy and to protect U.S. interests.*

Section 8   *(1990 & beyond)*

Entering a New Millennium

In 1990 the United States was one of the world's leading nations. Its resources and technology made it a leader in the production of goods and services. Its principles of freedom and opportunity provided its people with one of the world's highest standards of living.

The diverse population of the United States reflected the history of a nation settled by people from every part of the world. According to the 1990 census, most Americans lived throughout the country in large **metropolitan areas**, or cities surrounded by suburbs. They earned more money and lived longer than Americans in the past. In spite of widespread prosperity, however, many Americans lived in poverty.

As the United States enters a new millennium, it must consider ways to meet the needs of an aging population. It also faces challenges in a changing world. Defending human rights, supporting economic development, and protecting the environment have become global issues.

◄ *Skyscrapers tower over midtown Manhattan in New York – the largest U.S. city in population in 1990.*

Seattle, Washington, became an aerospace and technology center as well as a leading U.S. port for Pacific Rim trade. ▶

Did You Know ?

More than half the people who lived in the Los Angeles metropolitan area in 1990 moved there from other countries or other parts of the United States.

Population Distribution by Age, 1990

Age groups (vertical axis): 0-9, 10-19, 20-29, 30-39, 40-49, 50-59, 60-74, 75-84, 85+

Percent of population (horizontal axis): 5, 10, 15, 20

	1992	1992	1997
People	Mae Carol Jemison, of Illinois, becomes first African American woman to travel in space.	Ross Perot, of Texas, runs as independent candidate for President of the United States.	Madeleine Albright, who was born in Czechoslovakia, becomes first woman U.S. secretary of state.
	1991	**1992**	**1994**
Events	Collapse of the Soviet Union marks end of Cold War.	World leaders hold Earth Summit in Rio de Janeiro, Brazil.	United States, Canada, and Mexico sign North American Free Trade Agreement (NAFTA).
	1991	**1991**	**1993**
Literature	*There Are No Children Here*, by Alex Kotlowitz, describes social conditions in Chicago's inner city.	*The Lost Garden*, by Laurence Yep, describes how the author grew up as a Chinese American in San Francisco.	*Having Our Say*, by the Delany sisters, describes 100 years of African American life in North Carolina and New York, NY.

▲ *In 1990 the United States had more than 350 metropolitan areas. The largest of these areas are indicated in red on the map. Los Angeles-Long Beach had a 1990 population of almost 9 million, making it the country's largest metropolitan area in population.*

The United States

0   100   200   300   400 miles

| Cities and Towns | 0 to 50,000 | ○ | 500,000 to 1,000,000 | ◎ |
| | 50,000 to 500,000 | ⊙ | 1,000,000 and over | |

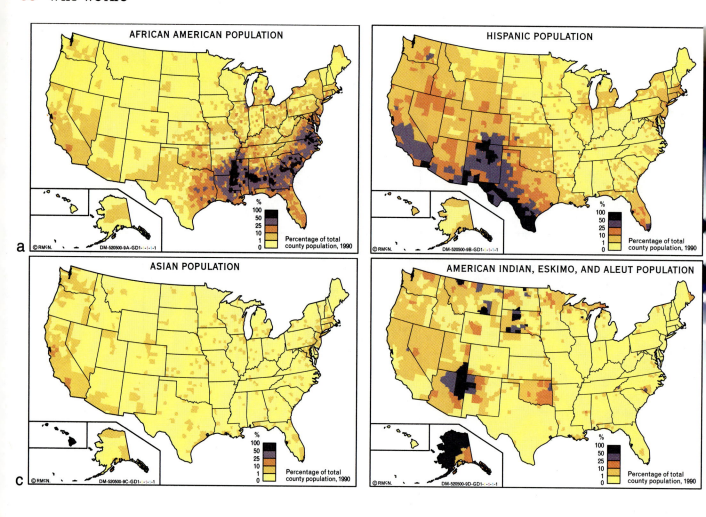

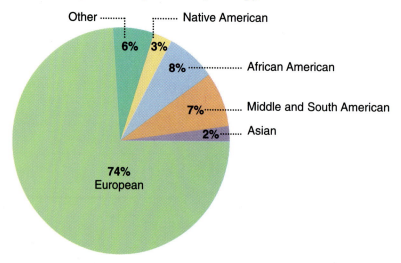

United States Population by Ancestry Group, 1990

Other
Native American
6% — 3%
8% ⋯⋯⋯ African American
7% ⋯⋯ Middle and South American
2% ⋯⋯ Asian
74% European

The maps show some major racial/ethnic groups in the United States in 1990 and where they lived. The graph shows the percentages of people of different ancestry groups within the United States population in 1990.

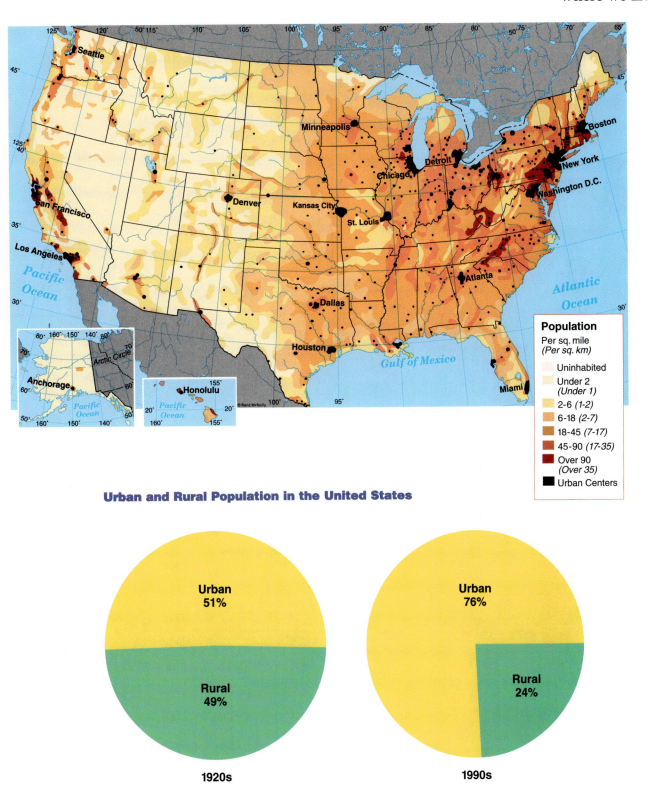

Urban and Rural Population in the United States

Urban 51%

Rural 49%

1920s

Urban 76%

Rural 24%

1990s

Population

Per sq. mile
(Per sq. km)

Uninhabited

Under 2
(Under 1)

2-6 *(1-2)*

6-18 *(2-7)*

18-45 *(7-17)*

45-90 *(17-35)*

Over 90
(Over 35)

Urban Centers

In 1990 more than three-fourths of all Americans lived in urban areas. The map shows the locations of the most densely populated parts of the United States. Notice that several metropolitan areas from Boston to Washington, D.C. had grown together to form a large, densely populated area called a megalopolis. The circle graphs compare the percentages of urban and rural population in the United States in the 1920s and 1990s.

Median Family Income, 1990

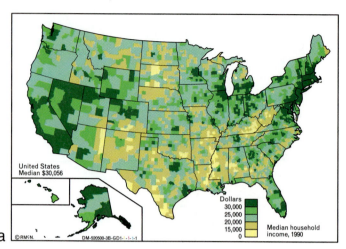

United States
Median $30,056

Dollars
30,000
25,000
20,000
15,000
0

Median household
income, 1990

©RM♀N.   DM-520500-3B-GD1- -l- l-1

a

▲ The map shows median family income, or the middle value of all family incomes, in different parts of the United States in 1990.

Lifetime Expectance, 1990

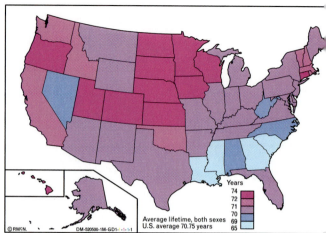

Years
74
72
71
70
69
65

Average lifetime, both sexes
U.S. average 70.75 years

©RM♀N.   DM-520500-1M-GD1- -l- l-1

▲ The map shows the average lifetime of all Americans in different parts of the United States in 1990.

Median Family Income (in current dollars), 1960-1990

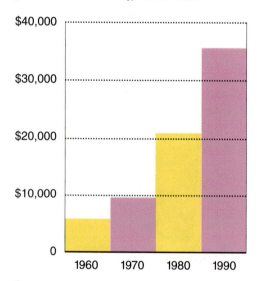

$40,000

$30,000

$20,000

$10,000

0

1960   1970   1980   1990

▲ The graph shows how median family income throughout the United States changed between 1960 and 1990.

Lifetime Expectance of Males and Females 1900-1990

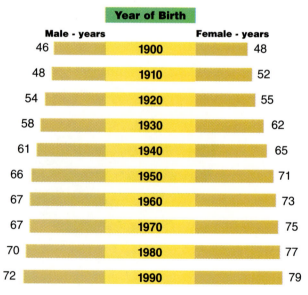

	Year of Birth	
Male - years		**Female - years**
46	1900	48
48	1910	52
54	1920	55
58	1930	62
61	1940	65
66	1950	71
67	1960	73
67	1970	75
70	1980	77
72	1990	79

▲ The graph shows how average lifetimes of males and females in the United States changed between 1900 and 1990.

Percentage of U.S. Population Below Poverty Level, 1990

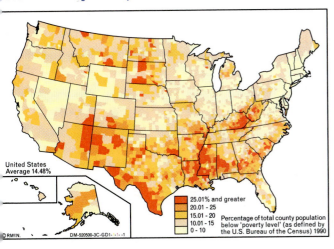

United States Average 14.48%

25.01% and greater
20.01 - 25
15.01 - 20
10.01 - 15
0 - 10

Percentage of total county population below 'poverty level' (as defined by the U.S. Bureau of the Census) 1990

©RMcN.   DM-520500-3C-GD1- -!- -

▲ The map shows the percentages of people living below the poverty level in different parts of the United States in 1990. Poverty level is based on the income needed to feed a family adequately without spending more than a third of the family income on food.

U.S. Unemployment Rates, 1990

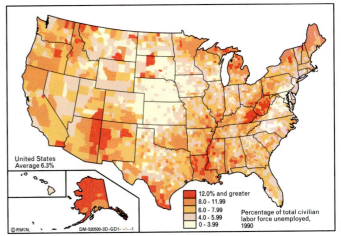

United States Average 6.3%

12.0% and greater
8.0 - 11.99
6.0 - 7.99
4.0 - 5.99
0 - 3.99

Percentage of total civilian labor force unemployed, 1990

©RMcN.   DM-520500-3D-GD1- -!- -

b

▲ The map shows the percentages of unemployed workers in different parts of the United States in 1990.

Percentage of U.S. Population Below Poverty Level, 1960-1990

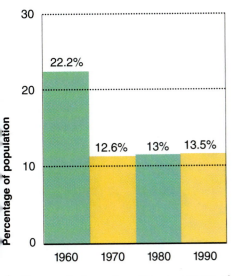

Percentage of population

22.2%   12.6%   13%   13.5%

1960   1970   1980   1990

▲ The graph shows how the percentage of Americans below the poverty level changed between 1960 and 1990.

U.S. Unemployment Rates, 1960-1990

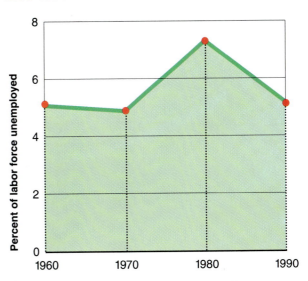

Percent of labor force unemployed

1960   1970   1980   1990

▲ The graph shows how the percentage of unemployed workers in the United States changed between 1960 and 1990.

The 50 states that make up the United States cover an area of more than 3 1/2 million square miles. The United States is the world's fourth largest country in area.

In 1990 the United States had a population of about 250 million. It was the world's third largest country in population.

Populations of United States Colonies and States, 1650-1990

States	1650	1700	1750	1770	1790	1800	1820	1840
Alabama							127,901	590,756
Alaska								
Arizona								
Arkansas							14,273	97,574
California								
Colorado								
Connecticut	4,139	25,970	111,280	183,881	237,946	251,002	275,248	309,978
Delaware	185	2,470	28,704	35,496	59,096	64,273	72,749	78,085
District of Columbia						8,144	23,336	33,745
Florida								54,477
Georgia			5,200	23,375	82,548	162,686	340,989	691,392
Hawaii								
Idaho								
Illinois							55,211	476,183
Indiana						5,641	147,178	685,866
Iowa								43,112
Kansas								
Kentucky				15,700	73,677	220,955	564,317	779,828
Louisiana							153,407	352,411
Maine[4]				31,257	96,540	151,719	298,335	501,793
Maryland	4,504	29,604	141,073	202,599	319,728	341,548	407,350	470,019
Massachusetts[4]	16,603	55,941	188,000	235,308	378,787	422,845	523,287	737,699
Michigan							8,896	212,267
Minnesota								
Mississippi						8,850	75,448	375,651
Missouri							66,586	383,702
Montana								
Nebraska								
Nevada								
New Hampshire	1,305	4,958	27,505	62,396	141,885	183,858	244,161	284,574
New Jersey		14,010	71,393	117,431	184,139	211,149	277,575	373,306
New Mexico								
New York	4,116	19,107	76,696	162,920	340,120	589,051	1,372,812	2,428,921
North Carolina		10,720	72,984	197,200	393,751	478,103	638,829	753,419
North Dakota[3]								
Ohio						45,365	581,434	1,519,467
Oklahoma[5]								
Oregon								
Pennsylvania		17,950	119,666	240,057	434,373	602,365	1,049,458	1,724,033
Rhode Island	785	5,894	33,226	58,196	68,825	69,122	83,059	108,830
South Carolina		5,704	64,000	124,244	249,073	345,591	502,741	594,398
South Dakota[3]								
Tennessee				1,000	35,691	105,602	422,823	829,210
Texas								
Utah								
Vermont				10,000	85,425	154,465	235,981	291,948
Virginia[6]	18,731	58,560	231,033	447,016	691,737	807,557	938,261	1,025,227
Washington								
West Virginia[6]					55,873	78,592	136,808	224,537
Wisconsin								30,945
Wyoming								
Total[1]	50,368	250,888	1,170,760	2,148,076	3,929,214	5,308,483	9,638,453	17,069,453[2]

[1] All figures prior to 1890 exclude Indians unaffected by the pioneer movement. Figures for 1650 through 1770 include only the British colonies that later became the United States. No areas are included prior to their annexation to the United States. However, many of the figures refer to territories prior to their admission as states. U.S. total includes Alaska from 1880 through 1970 and Hawaii from 1900 through 1970.

[2] U.S. total for 1840 includes 6,100 persons on public ships in service of the United States not credited to any state.

[3] South Dakota figure for 1860 represents entire Dakota Territory. North and South Dakota figures for 1880 are for the parts of Dakota Territory which later constituted the respective states.

1860	1880	1900	1920	1940	1950	1960	1970	1980	1990
964,201	1,262,505	1,828,697	2,348,174	2,832,961	3,061,743	3,266,740	3,444,165	3,893,888	4,062,608
	33,426	63,592	55,036	72,524	128,643	226,167	302,173	401,851	551,947
	40,440	122,931	334,162	499,261	749,587	1,302,161	1,772,482	2,718,425	3,677,985
435,450	802,525	1,311,564	1,752,204	1,949,387	1,909,511	1,786,272	1,923,295	2,286,435	2,362,239
379,994	864,694	1,485,053	3,426,861	6,907,387	10,586,223	15,717,204	19,953,134	23,667,565	29,839,250
34,277	194,327	539,700	939,629	1,123,296	1,325,089	1,753,947	2,207,259	2,889,735	3,307,912
460,147	622,700	908,420	1,380,631	1,709,242	2,007,280	2,535,234	3,032,217	3,107,576	3,295,669
112,216	146,608	184,735	223,003	266,505	318,085	446,292	548,104	594,317	668,696
75,080	177,624	278,718	437,571	663,091	802,178	763,956	756,510	638,432	609,909
140,424	269,493	528,542	968,470	1,897,414	2,771,305	4,951,560	6,789,443	9,746,342	13,003,362
1,057,286	1,542,180	2,216,331	2,895,832	3,123,723	3,444,578	3,943,116	4,589,575	5,463,105	6,508,419
		154,001	255,881	422,770	499,794	632,772	769,913	964,691	1,115,274
	32,610	161,772	431,866	524,873	588,637	667,191	713,008	944,038	1,011,986
1,711,951	3,077,871	4,821,550	6,485,280	7,897,241	8,712,176	10,081,158	11,113,976	11,426,596	11,466,682
1,350,428	1,978,301	2,516,462	2,930,390	3,427,796	3,934,224	4,662,498	5,193,669	5,490,260	5,564,228
674,913	1,624,615	2,231,853	2,404,021	2,538,268	2,621,073	2,757,537	2,825,041	2,913,808	2,787,424
107,206	996,096	1,470,495	1,769,257	1,801,028	1,905,299	2,178,611	2,249,071	2,364,236	2,485,600
1,155,684	1,648,690	2,147,174	2,416,630	2,845,627	2,944,806	3,038,156	3,219,311	3,660,257	3,698,969
708,002	939,946	1,381,625	1,798,509	2,363,880	2,683,516	3,257,022	3,643,180	4,206,312	4,238,216
628,279	648,936	694,466	768,014	847,226	913,774	969,265	993,663	1,125,027	1,233,223
687,049	934,943	1,188,044	1,449,661	1,821,244	2,343,001	3,100,689	3,922,399	4,216,975	4,798,622
1,231,066	1,783,085	2,805,346	3,852,356	4,316,721	4,690,514	5,148,578	5,689,170	5,737,037	6,029,051
749,113	1,636,937	2,420,982	3,668,412	5,256,106	6,371,766	7,823,194	8,875,083	9,262,078	9,328,784
172,023	780,773	1,751,394	2,387,125	2,792,300	2,982,483	3,413,864	3,805,069	4,075,970	4,387,029
791,305	1,131,597	1,551,270	1,790,618	2,183,796	2,178,914	2,178,141	2,216,912	2,520,638	2,586,443
1,182,012	2,168,380	3,106,665	3,404,055	3,784,664	3,954,653	4,319,813	4,677,399	4,916,759	5,137,804
	39,159	243,329	548,889	559,456	591,024	674,767	694,409	786,690	803,655
28,841	452,402	1,066,300	1,296,372	1,315,834	1,325,510	1,411,330	1,483,791	1,569,825	1,584,617
6,857	62,266	42,335	77,407	110,247	160,083	285,278	488,738	800,493	1,206,152
326,073	346,991	411,488	443,083	491,524	533,242	606,921	737,681	920,610	1,113,915
672,035	1,131,116	1,883,669	3,155,900	4,160,165	4,835,329	6,066,782	7,168,164	7,364,823	7,748,634
93,516	119,565	195,310	360,350	531,818	681,187	951,023	1,016,000	1,302,981	1,521,779
3,880,735	5,082,871	7,268,894	10,385,227	13,479,142	14,830,192	16,782,304	18,241,266	17,558,072	18,044,505
992,622	1,399,750	1,893,810	2,559,123	3,571,623	4,061,929	4,556,155	5,082,059	5,881,813	6,657,630
	36,909	319,146	646,872	641,935	619,636	632,446	617,761	652,717	641,364
2,339,511	3,198,062	4,157,545	5,759,394	6,907,612	7,946,627	9,706,397	10,652,017	10,797,624	10,887,325
		790,391	2,028,283	2,336,434	2,233,351	2,328,284	2,559,253	3,025,290	3,157,604
52,465	174,768	413,536	783,389	1,089,684	1,521,341	1,768,687	2,091,385	2,633,149	2,853,733
2,906,215	4,282,891	6,302,115	8,720,017	9,900,180	10,498,012	11,319,366	11,793,909	11,863,895	11,924,710
174,620	276,531	428,556	604,397	713,346	791,896	859,488	949,723	947,154	1,005,984
703,708	995,577	1,340,316	1,683,724	1,899,804	2,117,027	2,382,594	2,590,516	3,121,833	3,505,707
4,837	98,268	401,570	636,547	642,961	652,740	680,514	666,257	690,768	699,999
1,109,801	1,542,359	2,020,616	2,337,885	2,915,841	3,291,718	3,567,089	3,924,164	4,591,120	4,896,641
604,215	1,591,749	3,048,710	4,663,228	6,414,824	7,711,194	9,579,677	11,196,730	14,229,288	17,059,805
40,273	143,963	276,749	449,396	550,310	688,862	890,627	1,059,273	1,461,037	1,727,784
315,098	332,286	343,641	352,428	359,231	377,747	389,881	444,732	551,456	564,964
1,219,630	1,512,565	1,854,184	2,309,187	2,677,773	3,318,680	3,966,949	4,648,494	5,346,818	6,216,568
11,594	75,116	518,103	1,356,621	1,736,191	2,378,963	2,853,214	3,409,169	4,132,180	4,887,941
376,688	618,457	958,800	1,463,701	1,901,974	2,005,552	1,860,421	1,744,237	1,950,279	1,801,625
775,881	1,315,497	2,069,042	2,632,067	3,137,587	3,434,575	3,951,777	4,417,933	4,705,521	4,906,745
	20,789	92,531	194,402	250,742	290,529	330,066	332,416	469,557	455,975
31,443,321	**50,189,209**	**76,212,168**	**106,021,537**	**132,164,569**	**151,325,798**	**179,323,175**	**203,235,298**	**226,547,346**	**249,632,692**

[4]Maine figures for 1770 through 1800 are for that area of Massachusetts which became the state of Maine in 1820. Massachusetts figures exclude Maine from 1770 through 1800, but include it from 1650 through 1750. Massachusetts figure for 1650 also includes population of Plymouth (1,566), a separate colony until 1691.

[5]Oklahoma figure for 1900 includes population of Indian Territory (392,060).

[6]West Virginia figures for 1790 through 1860 are for that area of Virginia which became West Virginia in 1863. These figures are excluded from the figures for Virginia from 1790 through 1860.

Facts About the States

State	Admission to the Union date (order)	Capital	Area in sq.mi. (rank in area)	Nickname	Postal Abbreviation
Alabama	1819 (22)	Montgomery	51,705 (29)	The Heart of Dixie	AL
Alaska	1959 (49)	Juneau	591,004 (1)	Last Frontier	AK
Arizona	1912 (48)	Phoenix	114,000 (6)	Grand Canyon State	AZ
Arkansas	1836 (25)	Little Rock	53,187 (27)	Land of Opportunity	AR
California	1850 (31)	Sacramento	158,706 (3)	Golden State	CA
Colorado	1876 (38)	Denver	104,091 (8)	Centennial State	CO
Connecticut	1788 (5)	Hartford	5.018 (48)	Constitution State	CT
Delaware	1787 (1)	Dover	2,044 (49)	First State	DE
Florida	1845 (27)	Tallahassee	58,664 (22)	Sunshine State	FL
Georgia	1788 (4)	Atlanta	58,910 (21)	Empire State of the South	GA
Hawaii	1959 (50)	Honolulu	6,471 (47)	Aloha State	HI
Idaho	1890 (43)	Boise	83,564 (13)	Gem State	ID
Illinois	1818 (21)	Springfield	56,345 (24)	Land of Lincoln	IL
Indiana	1816 (19)	Indianapolis	36,185 (38)	Hoosier State	IN
Iowa	1846 (29)	Des Moines	56,275 (25)	Hawkeye State	IA
Kansas	1861 (34)	Topeka	82,277 (14)	Sunflower State	KS
Kentucky	1792 (15)	Frankfort	40,409 (37)	Bluegrass State	KY
Louisiana	1812 (18)	Baton Rouge	47,752 (31)	Pelican State	LA
Maine	1820 (23)	Augusta	33,265 (39)	Pine Tree State	ME
Maryland	1788 (7)	Annapolis	10,460 (42)	Old Line State	MD
Massachusetts	1788 (6)	Boston	8,284 (45)	Bay State	MA
Michigan	1837 (26)	Lansing	58,527 (23)	Wolverine State	MI
Minnesota	1858 (32)	St. Paul	84,402 (12)	Gopher State	MN
Mississippi	1817 (20)	Jackson	47,689 (32)	Magnolia State	MS
Missouri	1821 (24)	Jefferson City	69,697 (19)	Show Me State	MO

State	Admission to the Union date (order)	Capital	Area in sq.mi. (rank in area)	Nickname	Postal Abbreviation
Montana	1889 (41)	Helena	147,046 (4)	Treasure State	MT
Nebraska	1867 (37)	Lincoln	77,355 (15)	Cornhusker State	NE
Nevada	1864 (36)	Carson City	110,561 (7)	Silver State	NV
New Hampshire	1788 (9)	Concord	9,297 (44)	Granite State	NH
New Jersey	1787 (3)	Trenton	7,787 (46)	Garden State	NJ
New Mexico	1912 (47)	Santa Fe	121,593 (5)	Land of Enchantment	NM
New York	1788 (11)	Albany	49,108 (30)	Empire State	NY
North Carolina	1789 (12)	Raleigh	52,669 (28)	Tar Heel State	NC
North Dakota	1889 (39)	Bismarck	70,702 (17)	Flickertail State	ND
Ohio	1803 (17)	Columbus	41,330 (35)	Buckeye State	OH
Oklahoma	1907 (46)	Oklahoma City	69,956 (18)	Sooner State	OK
Oregon	1859 (33)	Salem	97,073 (10)	Beaver State	OR
Pennsylvania	1787 (2)	Harrisburg	45,308 (33)	Keystone State	PA
Rhode Island	1790 (13)	Providence	1,212 (50)	Ocean State	RI
South Carolina	1788 (8)	Columbia	31,113 (40)	Palmetto State	SC
South Dakota	1889 (40)	Pierre	77,116 (16)	Mount Rushmore State	SD
Tennessee	1796 (16)	Nashville	42,114 (34)	Volunteer State	TN
Texas	1845 (28)	Austin	266,807 (2)	Lone Star State	TX
Utah	1896 (45)	Salt Lake City	84,899 (11)	Beehive State	UT
Vermont	1791 (14)	Montpelier	9,614 (43)	Green Mountain State	VT
Virginia	1788 (10)	Richmond	40,767 (36)	Old Dominion	VA
Washington	1889 (42)	Olympia	68,139 (20)	Evergreen State	WA
West Virginia	1863 (35)	Charleston	24,231 (41)	Mountain State	WV
Wisconsin	1848 (30)	Madison	56,153 (26)	Badger State	WI
Wyoming	1890 (44)	Cheyenne	97,809 (9)	Equality State	WY

In addition to place names that appear on the maps in this atlas, the Index also lists names of people, groups, events, and other topics related to American history. It provides explanatory information, such as dates, identifications, and geographic locations for many entries. When appropriate, entries are cross-referenced to related topics.

The Index lists boldfaced page numbers on which each entry appears. A small letter beside a page number identifies a specific map on the page on which the entry appears. Postal abbreviations are used for state names.

The following abbreviations also are used:

Ft.	Fort	St.	Saint
g	graph	t	table
Is.	Islands	terr.	territory
p	photograph	U.S.	United States
pop.	population		

A

Acadia, **22b**
Addams, Jane, **45**
Adena (American Indians), **6**
African American Migration, *1940-1970,* **60**
Alabama, **37, 41, 42, 43, 44a**
Alamo, *TX battle site, 1836,* **34b, 36**
Alaska, **47a**
Albany, NY, **22a, 22b, 27a, 33a, 41**
Albright, Madeleine, **63**
Alcott, Louisa May, **6**
Algeria, **57**
Algonkian (American Indian language group), **16b**
Algonquin (American Indians), **11**
Allied Powers, *World War II,* **56, 57**
American Samoa, **47a**
Antietam, *MD battle site, 1862,* **43, 44b**
Anza, Juan Bautista de, **25**
Anzio, *Italy battle site, 1944,* **57**
Apache (American Indians), **11, 46**
Appomattox, *VA battle site, 1865,* **43, 44c**
Arab League, **58**
Arapahoe (American Indians), **11, 46**
Arawak (American Indians), **11**
Argonne Forest, *France battle site, 1918,* **50b**
Arkansas, **37, 41, 42, 43, 44a, 46**
Armstrong, Neil, **7**
Astoria, Oregon Country, **33b, 34a**
Atlanta, *GA battle site, 1864,* **43, 44a**
Atlantic, Battle of the, *1940-1943,* **55**
Axis Powers, *World War II,* **56, 57**
Aztec Empire, North America, **9, 11, 14**

B

Balboa, Vasco Núñez de, *route of, 1501-1513,* **14**
Baltimore, MD, **29b, 33a, 37, 41, 60**
Banneker, Benjamin, **25**
Bataan, *Philippines battle site, 1942,* **56**
battles. *See names of individual battles, individual wars.*
Bay of Pigs, *Cuba invasion, 1961,* **62**
Belgium, **50b, 57**
Belleau Wood, *France battle site, 1918,* **50b**
Bennington, *VT battle site, 1777,* **27a**
Bent's Fort, NE, **34a, 36**
Berthold Indian Reservation, **46**
Blackfeet (American Indians), **11**
Boston, MA, **19b, 19c, 22b, 24, 26a, 26b, 29b, 37, 41**
Bougainville, *New Guinea battle site, 1943,* **56**
Bradstreet, Anne, **17**
Brandywine, *PA battle site, 1777,* **27a**
Breuckelen, Dutch terr., **18b**
Bristol, England, **15a, 16a**
Britain, Battle of, *1940,* **55**
Brooklyn Heights, *NY battle site, 1776,* **26c**
Brulé, Étienne, *routes of, 1612-1623,* **16b**
Buena Vista, *Mexico battle site, 1847,* **34b**
Buffalo, NY, **33a, 37**
Bulge, Battle of the, *Belgium, 1944,* **57**
Bull Run, *VA battle site, 1861-1862, 43, 44b*
Bunker Hill, *MA battle site, 1775,* **26b**
Butterfield Overland Mail Route, **46**

C

C & O Canal, **35a**
Cabot, John, *routes of, 1497-1498,* **15a**
Cahokia, Northwest Territory, **21, 26d, 30**
California, **36, 40a, 41, 42, 46**
California Trail, **34a, 36**
Cambodia, **59b**
Camden, *SC battle site, 1780-1781,* **27b**
Cantigny, *France battle site, 1918,* **50b**
Cape Breton Island, Canada, **15a, 22b**
Cape Canaveral, FL, **51**
Cape Cod, MA, **16b, 19a, 19b, 19c**
Carib (American Indians), **11**
Caroline Islands, **54**
Cartier, Jacques, *routes of, 1534-1536,* **16a**
Cayuse (American Indians), **11**

Cayuga (American Indians), **11**
Champlain, Samuel de, *routes of, 1603-1615,* **16b**
Chancellorsville, *VA battle site, 1863,* **43, 44b**
Charleston, SC, **24a, 27b, 29b, 37, 41, 42, 44a**
Charlestown, MA, **26a**
Château-Thierry, *France battle site, 1918,* **50b**
Chattanooga, *TN battle site, 1863,* **43, 44a**
Cherokee (American Indians), **11, 20, 35b, 46**
Cheyenne (American Indians), **11, 46**
Chicago, IL, **37, 41, 43, 46, 60**
Chickamauga, *GA battle site, 1863,* **43, 44a**
Chickasaw (American Indians), **11, 20, 35b, 46**
Chickasaw Bluffs, *MS battle site, 1862,* **43**
Chihuahua, Mexico, **34b, 36**
China, **54, 56, 58, 59a**
Chinook (America Indians), **11**
Chippewa (American Indians), **11, 35b**
Chisholm Trail, **46**
Chocktaw (American Indians), **11, 35b, 46**
Cimarron Crossing Trail, **36–37**
Cincinnati, OH, **29b, 30, 32a, 33a, 41**
Civil War
    1861-1863, **44b**
    1861-1865, **43, 44a**
    1864-1865, **44c**
    See also names of individual battle sites.
Clark, George Rogers, *route of 1778-1779,* **26d**
Clark, William, **6**
Cleveland, OH, **33a, 60**
Cliff Palace, *Mesa Verde, CO,* **p9**
coal, *U.S. deposits, 1920,* **52**
Cody, Buffalo Bill, *WY monument,* **p45**
Cold Harbor, *VA battle site, 1864,* **43, 44c**
Colonies, Original British, **21, 29a, 29b**
Colorado, **46**
Colorado Territory, **42**
Columbia, *SC battle site, 1865,* **43**
Columbia & Colville Indian Reservation, **46**
Columbus, Christopher, *routes of, 1492-1502,* **14**
Comanche (American Indians), **11**
Compromise of 1850, **40a**
Concord, Battle of, *MA, 1775,* **26a**
Confederate States, *Civil War,* **42, 43**
Connecticut, **19c, 21, 22a, 22b, 24a, 26b, 27a, 29a, 29b, 33a, 35a, 37, 41, 42**
Connecticut Claim, **29a**

Connecticut Western Reserve, **29a**
Cooper, James Fenimore, **31**
Coral Sea, Battle of, *1942,* **54, 56**
Coronado, Francisco, *route of,
    1540-1542,* **14**
Cortés, Hernando, *route of, 1519,* **14**
cotton, *U.S. production of, 1820-1860,*
    41
Cowpens, *SC battle site, 1781,* **27b**
Cree (American Indians), **11**
Creek (American Indians), **11, 20,
    35b, 46**
Crèvecoeur, Jean de, **25**
Crow (American Indians), **11, 46**
Cuba, **47b, 62**
Cuban Missile Crisis, *1962,* **62**
Cumberland Road, **35a, 37**
Cuzco, Inca Empire, **14**

D

DaGama, Vasco, *routes of, 1498,* **13**
Dakota Territory, **42**
Dallas, TX, **46, 60**
Da Nang, South Vietnam, **59b**
Dare, Virginia, **9**
Davis, John, *routes of, 1585-1586,* **15b**
D-Day, *Normandy, France battle site,
    1944,* **57**
Delany sisters, **63**
Delaware, **21, 22a, 22b, 24a, 27a,
    29a, 29b, 33a, 35a, 37, 41, 42,
    43**
Delaware (American Indians), **11, 35b**
Demilitarized Zone (DMZ), Vietnam,
    59b
Denver, CO, **46**
DeSoto, Hernando, *route of,
    1539-1542,* **14**
Detroit, MI, **20, 26d, 30, 33a, 60**
Devils Lake Indian Reservation, **46**
Dias, Bartholomeu, *routes of, 1488,* **13**
Dodge City, KS, **46**
Dominican Republic, **62**
Durham Station, *NC battle site, 1865*
    44a
Dust Bowl, **53**

E

economy, *colonial,* **24a**
    *See also industry, names of indi-
    vidual products.*
Egypt, **57**
El Alamein, *Egypt battle site, 1942,* **57**
El Caney, *Cuba battle site, 1898,* **47b**
El Paso, TX, **34b**
El Salvador, **62**
employment, *U.S. rates, 1960-1990,*
    g69
Empress Augusta Bay, *Solomon Is.
    battle site, 1943,* **56**
Eniwetok, *Marshall Is. battle site,
    1944,* **56**
Ericson, Leif, **9**
Erie, PA, **33a**
Erie Canal, **31, 35a**
Europe, *World War I,* **50a, 50b**

Europe, *World War II,* **55, 57**
European Economic Community
    (EEC), **58**
expansion *See United States,
    expansion.*
exploration routes *See names of
    individual explorers.*

F

Fallen Timbers, *Northwest Territory
    battle site, 1794,* **29b, 32a**
First Americans, *routes of,* **10a**
Five Forks, *VA battle site, 1865,* **44c**
Flathead Indian Reservation, **46**
Florida, **37, 41, 42, 43**
forests, *colonial,* **24a**
Ft. Atkinson, Nebraska Territory, **37**
Ft. Boise, Oregon Country, **34a**
Ft. Bridger, Utah Territory, **34a, 36**
Ft. Casimir, Dutch terr., **18b**
Ft. Christina, *site of Wilmington, DE,*
    18b
Ft. Clatsop, Oregon Country, **32b**
Ft. Crèvecoeur, French terr., **20, 22a**
Ft. Crown Point, NY, **20, 22a, 22b,
    26b, 27a**
Ft. Cumberland, MD, **22a**
Ft. des Miamis, French terr., **20**
Ft. Detroit, French terr., **22a**
Ft. Donelson, *TN battle site, 1862,* **43,
    44a**
Ft. Duquesne, French terr., **20, 22a,
    22b**
Ft. Dutchman's Point, NY, **32a**
Ft. Frontenac, French terr., **22a, 22b**
Ft. Greenville, Northwest Territory, **32a**
Ft. Hall, Oregon Territory, **34a, 36**
Ft. Hall Indian Reservation, **46**
Ft. Henry, *TN battle site, 1862,* **43, 44a**
Ft. Jefferson, FL, **42**
Ft. Kearney, Nebraska Territory, **34a, 36**
Ft. La Présentation, French terr., **20**
Ft. Laramie, Nebraska Territory, **34a, 36**
Ft. Lawrence, British terr., **22b**
Ft. Leavenworth, Kansas Territory, **37**
Ft. Le Boeuf, French terr., **22a**
Ft. Loudon, French terr., **20**
Ft. Mackinac, Michigan Territory, **30,
    32a, 33a**
Ft. Mandan, ND, **32b, 36**
Ft. McHenry, MD, **33a**
Ft. Miami, Northwest Territory, **32a**
Ft. Michilimackinac, French terr., **20,
    22a**
Ft. Monroe, VA, **42**
Ft. Nassau, *site of Philadelphia, PA,*
    18b
Ft. Necessity, French terr., **20, 22a,
    22b**
Ft. Niagara, NY, **20, 22a, 22b, 29b, 30,
    32a**
Ft. Ontario, NY, **29b**
Ft. Orange, Dutch settlement, **18b**
Ft. Oswegatchie, NY, **29b, 32a**
Ft. Oswego, NY, **20, 22a, 22b, 27a,
    32a**

Ft. Pickens, FL, **42**
Ft. Pitt, PA, **26d**
Ft. Point-au-Fer, NY, **32a**
Ft. Pontchartrain, French terr., **20**
Ft. Presqu'Isle, French terr., **20, 22a**
Ft. Prince George, English terr., **20**
Ft. Pulaski, *GA battle site, 1862,* **43**
Ft. Rouillé, French terr., **20**
Ft. Sandusky, French terr., **20, 22a**
Ft. Sault Ste. Marie, French terr., **20**
Ft. Scott, GA, **33b**
Ft. Snelling, Minnesota Territory, **37**
Ft. Stanton Indian Reservation, **46**
Ft. Stanwix, NY, **27a**
Ft. Sumter, *SC battle site, 1861,* **42, 43,
    44a**
Ft. Taylor, FL, **42**
Ft. Ticonderoga, NY, **22b, 26b, 27a**
Ft. Toulouse, French terr., **20**
Ft. Union, New Mexico Territory, **42**
Ft. Union, ND, **36**
Ft. Vancouver, Oregon Territory, **34a,
    36**
Ft. Venango, French terr., **20, 22a**
Ft. Vincennes, French terr., **20, 22a**
Ft. Wagner, *SC battle site, 1863,* **43**
Ft. Washington, NY, **26c**
Ft. Wayne, Northwest Territory, **32a**
Ft. William Henry, NY, **22a, 22b**
Fox (American Indians), **11**
France, **16a, 50a, 50b, 57**
Franklin, Benjamin, **17**
Fredericksburg, *VA battle site, 1862,*
    43, 44b
Freeman's Farm, *NY battle site, 1777,*
    27a
Fremont, John C., *routes of,* **34a**
French and Indian War, **22b**
Frobisher, Martin, *routes of, 1576-
    1578,* **15b**
frontiers, *U.S., 1860-1890,* **46**

G

Galarza, Ernesto, **51**
Gazala, *Libya battle site, 1942,* **57**
Georgia, **21, 24a, 27b, 29a, 29b, 37,
    41, 42, 43, 44a**
Georgia Claim, **29a**
Germantown, *PA battle site, 1777,* **27a**
Germany, **50a, 50b, 57**
Gettysburg, *PA battle site, 1863,* **p39,
    43, 44b**
Great Britain, **50b, 57**
Great Depression, *1929-1939,* **53**
Greenville, Treaty of, *1795,* **32a**
Grenada, **62**
Grey, Zane, **45**
gross domestic product, *1920–1990,*
    g51
Gros Ventre & Blackfeet Indian
    Reservation, **46**
Guadalcanal, *Solomon Is. battle site,
    1942-1943,* **54, 56**
Guam, **47a, 54, 56**
Guilford Courthouse, *NC battle site,
    1781,* **27b**

Haley, Alex, **7**
Halifax, Nova Scotia, **22b**
Hamilton, Alexander, **25**
Ha Noi, North Vietnam, **59b**
Havana, Cuba, **47b, 62**
Hawaii, **47a, 54**
Hawthorne, Nathaniel, **39**
Hiroshima, Japan, **56**
Hochelaga, *site of Montreal, Canada,*
    16a, 16b
Ho Chi Minh Trail, **59b**
Hollandia, *New Guinea battle site,*
    1944, **56**
Holly Springs, *MS battle site, 1862,* **43**
Honduras, **62**
Hopi (American Indians), **11**
Houston, TX, **46, p51, 60**
Hudson's Bay Company, **20, 23, 29b**
Huron (American Indians), **11, 16b**

I

Idaho, **46**
Illinois, **35a, 37, 41, 42, 43, 46**
Illinois (American Indians), **11**
immigration
    U.S., 1820-1870, **38**
    U.S., 1860-1919, **g45**
    U.S., 1880-1920, **48**
    U.S., 1910, **49**
    U.S., 1960s-1990s, **61**
Inca Empire, South America, **11, 14**
Inchon, South Korea, **59a**
income
    U.S., median family, 1960-1990, **g68**
    U.S., 1990, **68a**
Independence, MO, **34a, 40b**
Independence Rock, Nebraska
    Territory, **34a**
Indiana, **35a, 37, 41, 42, 43, 46**
Indians *See Native Americans.*
Indian Territory, **35−36, 40b, 41, 43,**
    46
indigo, *colonial production of,* **24a**
industry, *U.S., 1920,* **52**
Inuit, **11**
Iowa, **37, 41, 42, 43, 46**
iron, *U.S. production of, 1920,* **52**
ironworks, *colonial,* **24a**
Iroquois (American Indians), **11, 16b,**
    20
Irving, Washington, **31**
Italy, **57**
Iwo Jima
    Japan battle site, 1945, **56**
    monument, **p51**

J

Jackson, *MS battle site, 1863,* **43**
Jackson, Helen Hunt, **45**
Jalapa, Mexico, **34b**
Jamestown, Virginia Company, **18a**
Jay, John, **25**
Jefferson, Thomas, **31**
Jemison, Mae Carol, **63**
Joliet, Louis, *routes of, 1673,* **20**

Joseph, *Nez Percé chief,* **45**

K

Kansa Indian Reservation, **35b**
Kansas, **42, 43, 46**
Kansas Territory, **40b, 41**
Kansas-Nebraska Act, *1854,* **40b**
Kaskaskia, Northwest Territory, **20, 21,**
    26d, 30
Kasserine Pass, *Tunisia battle site,*
    1943, **57**
Kentucky, **29b, 32a, 35a, 37, 41, 42,**
    43, 44a
Khe Sanh, South Vietnam, **59b**
Kickapoo Indian Reservation, **35b**
King, Martin Luther, Jr., **51**
Kings Mountain, *SC battle site, 1780,*
    27b
Kiska and Attu Is., *AK battle site,*
    1942, **56**
Kittery, NH, **19c**
Klamath Indian Reservation, **46**
Knight, Sarah Kemble, **6**
Korean War, *1950,* **59a**
Kotlowitz, Alex, **63**
Kwajalein, *Marshall Is. battle site,*
    1944, **56**
Kwakiutl (American Indians), **11**

L

Lake Traverse Indian Reservation, **46**
land claims
    North America, 1763, **23**
    North America, 1783, **28a**
Laos, **59b**
La Salle, Robert Cavelier, Sieur de, **17,**
    20
Las Casas, Bartolomé de, **9**
Lassen's Trail, **36**
Lee, Harper, **51**
Lee, Robert E., **39**
Lewis, Meriwether, **6**
Lewis, Meriwether and Clark, William,
    routes of, 1804-1806, **32b, 36**
Lexington, Battle of, *MA, 1775,* **26a**
Leyte Gulf, *Philippines battle site,*
    1944, **56**
Libya, **57**
lifetime expectance, U.S.
    1900-1990, **g68**
    1990, **68b**
Lincoln, Abraham, **39**
Lindbergh, Charles, **51**
Little Big Horn, *MT battle site, 1876,*
    46
London Company, **18a**
Los Angeles, CA, **32b, 34a, 34b, 36,**
    41, 49, 60
Louisbourg, French terr., **22b**
Louisiana, **37, 41, 42, 43, 46**
Louisiana Purchase, *1803,* **32b, 36−37**

M

Madison, James, **25**
Maine, **35a, 37, 41, 42**

Malheur Indian Reservation, **46**
Manchester, NH, **27a**
Mandan (American Indians), **11, 32b**
Manhattan Island, Dutch terr., **18b**
Manila Bay, *Philippines battle site,*
    1898, **47c**
Marquette, Jacques, *routes of,* **20**
Marshall Islands, **54**
Maryland, **21, 22a, 22b, 24a, 27a,**
    27c, 29a, 29b, 33a, 35a, 37, 41,
    42, 43, 44b, 44c
Massachusetts, **19c, 21, 22a, 22b,**
    24a, 26b, 27a, 29b, 33a, 35a, 37,
    41, 42
Massachusetts & New York Claim, **29a**
Massachusetts Bay Colony, **19b**
Massachusetts Claim, **29a**
Matamoros, Mexico, **34b**
Maya Empire, North America, **11**
Mexican Cession, *1848,* **36**
Mexican War, *1846-1848,* **34b, 36−37**
Mexico, **34a, 34b**
Mexico City, Mexico, **14, 28b, 34b**
Miami (American Indians), **11, 35b**
Michigan, **37, 41, 42**
Michigan Territory, **33a**
Midway Islands, **47a, 54, 56**
Mile Run, *VA battle site, 1863,* **43**
mining, *U.S., 1860-1890,* **46**
Minnesota, **41, 42, 46**
Minnesota Territory, **36−37, 40a, 40b**
Minuit, Peter, **17**
missions, *Spanish, late 1700s,* **28b**
Mississippi, **37, 41, 42, 43, 44a, 46**
Mississippi Territory, **29b**
Missouri, **37, 41, 42, 43, 44a, 46**
Mobile Bay, *AL battle site, 1864,* **44a**
Modoc (American Indians), **11**
Mohave (American Indians), **11**
Mohawk (American Indians), **11**
Monitor versus *Merrimac, naval*
    battle, 1862, **44b**
Montana, **46**
Monterey, CA, **28b, 34a, 34b, 36**
Monterrey, Mexico, **34b, 36**
Montreal, Canada, **20, 22a, 22b, 26b,**
    27a, 29b, 33a
Mormon Trail, **34a, 36−37**
Morristown, NJ, **26c, 27a**
Mott, Lucretia, **31**
Murfreesboro, *TN battle site, 1862,* **43**
My Lai, South Vietnam, **59b**

N

Nashville, *TN battle site, 1864,* **44a**
National Road, **35a**
    See also Cumberland Road.
Native Americans
    homelands, **11**
    removal of, 1840, **35b**
    reservations, about 1840, **35b**
    reservations, 1880 **46**
    See also names of individual
        peoples; names of reservations.
Nauvoo, IL, **34a, 37**
Navajo (American Indians), **11, 46**
naval stores, *colonial,* **24a**

Nebraska, **46**
Nebraska Territory, **40b, 41, 42**
Nevada, **46**
Nevada Territory, **42**
New Amsterdam, *site of New York, NY,* **18b, 19c**
Newark, NJ, **26c, 60**
New Bedford, MA, **24a**
New Caledonia, **54**
New England, Council for, **19b**
Newfoundland, **10b, 15a, 16a, 28a**
New Gothenburg, Swedish terr., **18b**
New Hampshire, **19c, 21, 22a, 22b, 24a, 26b, 27a, 29a, 29b, 33a, 35a, 37, 41, 42**
New Jersey, **21, 22a, 22b, 24a, 26c, 27a, 29a, 33a, 35a, 37, 41, 42, 43**
New Mexico Territory, **37, 40a, 40b, 41, 42**
New Orleans, LA, **20, 28b, 29b, 32b, 33b, 37, 41, 43, 46**
New Spain, Viceroyalty of, **14**
New Town, MA, **19c**
New Utrecht, Dutch terr., **18b**
New York, **21, 22a, 22b, 24a, 26b, 26c, 27a, 29a, 29b, 32a, 33a, 35a, 37, 41, 42**
New York, NY, **22b, 24a, 26c, 27a, 29b, 33a, 33b, 37, 41, 60, p63**
New York Indians Reservation, **35b**
Nez Percé (American Indians), **11**
Nicaragua, **62**
Norfolk, VA, **24a, 41**
North America
    land claims, 1763, **23**
    land claims, 1783, **28a**
North Atlantic Treaty Organization (NATO) members, **58**
North Carolina, **21, 24a, 27b, 29a, 29b, 35a, 37, 41, 42, 43, 44a**
North Carolina Claim, **29a**
North Dakota, **46**
North Vietnam, **59b**
Northwest Passage, *search for, 1576-1586,* **15b**
Northwest Territory, **29b, 30**
Norway, **10b,**
Nova Scotia, **10b, 22b**

O

Oakland, CA, **60**
O'Connor, Sandra Day, **51**
Ohio, **33a, 35a, 37, 41, 42, 43**
oil, *U.S. production of, 1920,* **52**
Okinawa, *Japan battle site, 1945,* **56**
Old North Bridge, *MA battle site, 1775,* **26a**
Old Spanish Trail, **36**
Omaha, NE, **41, 46**
Oneida (American Indians), **11, 35b**
Onondaga (American Indians), **11**
Oregon, **41, 42, 46**
Oregon Country, **32b, 33b, 34a, 36**
Oregon Territory, **36, 40a**
Oregon Trail, **p31, 34a, 36**

Organization of American States (OAS), **58**
Organization of the Petroleum Exporting Countries (OPEC), **58**
Oriskany, *NY battle site, 1777,* **27a**
Osage Indian Reservation, **35b**
Ottawa (American Indians), **11, 35b**
Overland Stage Route, **46**

P

Paiute (American Indians), **11**
Panama, **62**
Panama Canal Zone, **47a, 62**
Panmunjom, South Korea, **59a**
Parks, Rosa, **7**
Pawnee (American Indians), **32b**
Pearl Harbor, HI, **7, 54**
Pecos Trail, **46**
Pennsylvania, **21, 22a, 22b, 24a, 27a, 29a, 29b, 32a, 33a, 35a, 37, 41, 42, 43, 44b**
Pequot (American Indians), **11**
Perot, Ross, **63**
Perryville, *KY battle site, 1862,* **44a**
Peru, Viceroyalty of, **14**
Petersburg, *VA battle site, 1864-1865,* **44c**
Philadelphia, PA, **22a, 22b, 24a, 27a, 29b, 33a, 37, 41, 43, 60**
Philippines, **47a, 47c, 54, 56**
Philippine Sea, *battle site, 1944,* **56**
Pike, Zebulon, *route of, 1806-1807,* **32b**
Pilgrims, **19a**
Pine Bluff, *AR battle site, 1863,* **44a**
Pizarro, Francisco, *route of, 1531-1533,* **14**
Plattsburg, *NY battle site, 1812,* **33a**
Pleiku, South Vietnam, **59b**
Plymouth, MA, **19b, 19c**
Plymouth Colony, *1620,* **19a**
Plymouth Company, **18a**
Pocahontas, **17**
Polo, Marco, **9**
Pomo (American Indians), **11**
Ponce de León, Juan, *route of, 1513,* **14**
Pony Express Route, **46**
Popham Colony, Plymouth Company, **18a**
population
    colonial, by national origin, 1790, **g25**
    colonial, growth of, 1650-1770, **g17**
    Native American, 1492, **g9**
    of colonies and states, 1650-1900, **t72**
    U.S. by ancestry group, 1990, **g66**
    U.S. density, **67**
    U.S. distribution by age, **g63**
    U.S. percent below poverty level, 1960-1990, **g69**
    U.S. urban and rural, 1920s and 1990s, **g67**
Port Gibson, *MS battle site, 1863,* **43**
Port Hudson, *LA battle site, 1863,* **44a**
Port Royal, Nova Scotia, **16b, 22b**

Port Royal, *SC battle site, 1861,* **43**
Portsmouth, RI, **19c**
Potawatomi Indian Reservation, **35b**
Powell, Colin, **7**
Powhatan (American Indians), **11**
Princeton, NJ, **26c**
Proclamation of 1763, Line of, **23**
Providence, RI, **19c, 29b**
Puerto Rico, **23, 28a, 47a, 62**

Q

Quebec, Canada, **16b, 20, 22b, 26b, 29b**

R

railroads
    U.S., 1820-1860, **41**
    U.S., 1850, **37**
    U.S., 1890, **46**
    U.S., 1920, **52**
Red Lake Indian Reservation, **46**
Revere, Paul, *route of, 1775,* **26a**
Revolutionary War
    Battles of Lexington and Concord, 1775-1776, **26a**
    in New England, 1775-1776, **26b**
    in the North, **27a**
    in the South, **27b**
    Final Campaign, 1781, **27c**
Rhode Island, **19c, 21, 22a, 22b, 24a, 26b, 29a, 29b, 33a, 35a, 37, 41, 42**
rice
    colonial production of, **24a**
    U.S. production of, 1820-1860, **41**
Richmond, VA, **29b, 44b, 44c**
Roanoke Island, London Company, **18a**
Rolfe, John, **17**
Roosevelt, Franklin, **6**
Roosevelt, Theodore, **45**
routes *See names of individual explorers, names of trails.*

S

Saigon, South Vietnam, **59b**
St. Augustine, FL, **6, 14**
St. Louis, MO, **30, 32b, 33b, 34a, 37, 41, 43, 46**
St. Mihiel, *France battle site, 1918,* **50b**
St. Tropez, *France battle site, 1944,* **57**
Saipan, *Mariana Is. battle site, 1944,* **56**
Salem, MA, **19b, 19c, 24a**
Salerno Beach, *Italy battle site, 1943,* **57**
San Antonio, TX, **28b, 36, 41**
San Diego, CA, **28b, 34b, 36**
San Francisco, CA, **28b, 32b, 34a, 36, 41**
San Jacinto, *TX battle site, 1847,* **34b**
San Juan Hill, *Cuba battle site, 1898,* **47b**
Santa Fe, New Mexico Territory, **28b, 32b, 34a, 34b, 36, 41**

80 Santa Fe Trail, **34a, 36**
Saratoga, *NY battle site, 1777,* **27a**
Sauk (American Indians), **11**
Savannah, GA, **24a, 41, 43, 44a**
Secession, *1860-1861,* **42**
Seattle, WA, **p63**
Seminole (American Indians), **11, 35b**
Seneca (American Indians), **11**
Seoul, South Korea, **59a**
Serra, Junípero, **6**
settlement
   U.S., 1775, **29a**
   U.S., 1800, **29b**
   U.S., 1820-1850, **37**
   See also Colonies, Original British.
settlements, Dutch & Swedish, *1623-1643,* **18b**
Seven Days Battle, *VA battle site, 1862,* **43, 44b**
Shawnee (American Indians), **11, 20, 35b**
Shenandoah Valley, *VA battle site, 1864,* **44c**
Shiloh, *TN battle site, 1862,* **43, 44a**
shipbuilding, *colonial,* **24a**
Shoshone (American Indians), **32b**
Sicily, *Invasion of, 1943,* **57**
Sioux (American Indians), **11, 35b, 46**
slave revolts, *U.S., 1820-1860,* **41**
slave states
   U.S., 1820-1860, **41**
   U.S., 1850, **40a**
   U.S., about 1860, **40c**
   U.S., 1860-1861, **42**
Smith, John, **6**
Solomon Islands, **54**
South Carolina, **21, 24a, 27b, 29a, 29b, 35a, 37, 41, 42, 43, 44a**
South Carolina Claim, **29a**
South Dakota, **46**
South Pass, Oregon Trail, **34a**
South Vietnam, **59b**
Soviet Union, **57**
Spanish-American War, *1898,* **47b, 47c**
Spotsylvania Court House, *VA battle site, 1864,* **44c**
Stanton, Elizabeth Cady, **31**
Staten Island, NY, **18b, 26c**
Statue of Liberty, **p45**
Steinbeck, John, **51**
Stillwater, *NY battle site, 1777,* **27a**
Stockbridge Indian Reservation, **35b**
Stone Mountain, *GA monument,* **p39**
Stowe, Harriet Beecher, **39**
sugar, *U.S. production of, 1820-1860,* **41**
Sutter's Fort, CA, **36**
Swaanendael, Dutch terr., **18b**

T
Taino (American Indians), **11**
Tampico, Mexico, **34b**
Tan, Amy, **7**
Tarawa, *Gilbert Is. battle site, 1943,* **56**
Tennessee, **29b, 35a, 37, 41, 42, 43, 44a, 46**
Tenochtitlán, Aztec Empire, **14**

territorial growth, U.S.
   See expansion, frontiers
Texas, **34b, 36, 40a, 41, 43, 46**
textiles, *U.S. production of,* **52**
Thoreau, Henry David, **31**
Tlingit (American Indians), **11**
tobacco
   colonial production of, **24a**
   U.S. production of, 1820-1860, **41**
Tobruk, *Libya battle site, 1942,* **57**
Tonkin, Gulf of, *battle site, 1964,* **59b**
Topeka, Kansas Territory, **40b, 41**
Tordesillas, Treaty of, *Line of Demarcation, 1494,* **14**
Toronto, Canada, **33a**
trade, *international, 1350-1450,* **12**
trade routes, *Atlantic Ocean, 1770,* **24b**
Trenton, *NJ battle site, 1776,* **26c**
Truk Islands, *battle site, 1944,* **56**
Tubman, Harriet, **39**
Tunis, *Tunisia battle site, 1943,* **57**
Tuscarora (American Indians), **11**
Twain, Mark, **45**

U
Uinta Indian Reservation, **46**
Underground Railroad, *about 1860,* **40c**
Union States, *Civil War,* **42**
United States, **64**
   1783, **28a**
   1819, **33b**
   1850, **40a**
   African American population, 1990, **66a**
   Amer. Indian, Eskimo & Aleut pop., 1990, **66d**
   area of selected lands added, 1803-1867, **g31**
   Asian population, 1990, **66c**
   expansion, 1800-1850, **37**
   expansion, 1830-about 1840, **34a**
   expansion, 1860-1890, **46**
   expansion, 1865-1920, **47a**
   facts about states, **t74**
   facts and world comparisons, **inside front cover**
   Hispanic population, 1990, **66b**
   poverty, 1990, **69a**
   unemployment, 1929-1939, **53**
   unemployment, 1990, **69b**
   See also names of individual states, employment, immigration, income, industry, lifetime expectance.
Utah Territory, **36, 40a, 40b, 41, 42**

V
Valley Forge, PA, **24a, 27a**
Vancouver Island, Oregon Country, **34a**
Vermont, **29a, 29b, 33a, 35a, 37, 41, 42**
Verrazano, Giovanni da, *routes of, 1524,* **16a**
Vespucci, Amerigo, **9**

Vicksburg, *MS battle site, 1863,* **43, 44a**
Vietnam War, *1957-1975,* **59b**
Vikings, *routes of, A.D. 1000,* **10b**
Vincennes, Northwest Territory, **26d, 29b, 30, 32a**
Virginia, **21, 22a, 22b, 24a, 27c, 29a, 29b, 33a, 35a, 37, 41, 42, 43, 44b**
Virginia Claim, **29a**
Virginia Company, **18a, 19b**
Virgin Islands, **47a**
voyages *See names of individual explorers.*

W
Wake Island, **47a, 54, 56**
Wampanoag (American Indians), **11**
war, *American deaths in,* **g39** *See also names of individual wars.*
War of 1812, **33a**
Warm Springs Indian Reservation, **46**
Washington, **46**
Washington, DC, **33a, 33b, 37, 41, 43, 44b, 44c, 60**
Washington, George, **25**
Washington Territory, **41, 42, 46**
Western Trail, **46**
West Virginia, **43, 44a**
whaling ports, *colonial,* **24a**
wheat, *colonial,* **24a**
Wheatley, Phillis, **25**
White Mountain Indian Reservation, **46**
White Plains, *NY battle site, 1776,* **26c**
Whitman, Walt, **39**
Wichita (American Indians), **11**
Wilder, Laura Ingalls, **7**
Wilderness, Battle of the, French terr., *1755,* **22a**
Wilderness, The, *VA battle site, 1864,* **43, 44c**
Wind River & Shoshone Indian Reservation, **46**
Wisconsin, **37, 41, 42, 46**
World
   1957-1975, **58**
   present, political, **70**
World War I, **50a, 50b**
World War II, **54, 56, 57**
Wounded Knee, SD, **51**
Wyandot Indian Reservation, **35b**
Wyoming, **46**

Y
Yakima Indian Reservation, **46**
Yep, Laurence, **63**
Yorktown
   VA battle site, 1781, **27c**
   VA battle site, 1862, **44b**
Young, Brigham, **31**

Z
Zuni (American Indians), **11**